THE LORD IS A WARRIOR

Ulf Ekman

The Lord is a warrior;
The Lord is his name.
Exodus 15:3

Word of Life Publications

THE LORD IS A WARRIOR

ISBN 91 7866 405 5

Original Swedish edition, copyright © 1995 Ulf Ekman.
All rights reserved

English translation, copyright © 2000 Ulf Ekman

Cover design, Gustav Magnusson

Printed in Finland by WS Bookwell, Finland 2000

Acknowledgments
Unless otherwise indicated, Scripture quotations are
from the *New King James Version* of the Bible, copyright
© 1979, 1980, 1982 Thomas Nelson Publishers, Inc. Used
by permission

Scripture quotations noted NIV are from the *Holy Bible, New
International Version,* copyright © 1973, 1978, 1984
International Bible Society. Used by permission of Zondervan
Bible Publishers

Table of Contents

Foreword

Teaching about spiritual warfare has been neglected in the body of Christ. Ignorance of the spiritual battle has caused a lot of damage for many believers. If one does not understand the battle that is going on in the spirit world, around every believer and the church, defeat will be more prevalent than victory. But, praise the name of the Lord, through the victory Jesus won on Calvary for every believer, we have the victory today. We are, as Romans 8:37 says, "more than conquerors".

As believers, we have been given a position of victory, but that position has to be lived out and made manifest in our lives. This is why the Bible talks both about a victory that has been won (Col 2:15) and the victory which is to be won (Eph 6:12). The unwillingness to see that there is a battle to fight has resulted in many believers not learning how to use their spiritual weapons. This book is for you who are tired of living in defeat, want to live in victory and are prepared to pay the price to stand against Satan until he gives way and there is a breakthrough.

Throughout the church history, spiritual warfare has been well-known. In classical Christian faith, it was talked of *ecclesia militans* and *ecclesia triumfans*, that is "the fighting church" and "the triumphant church".

The Gospel is a spiritual gospel. Its origin, purpose, goal and means are spiritual. The battle for the Gospel is fought with spiritual, not carnal weapons (2 Cor 10:3-5). Other religions try to spread their teachings in various ways. Some use the physical sword. Islam has its "holy" war—*Jihad*—in which its teachings are spread with threats, hate and violence. The Gospel is never like that. When Jesus came to earth, to *"destroy the works of the devil"*

5

(1 Joh 3:8), He did not come with physical armies and weapons.

God's weapon is His love to a lost mankind.

God's weapon is the anointing, revelation and power of the Holy Spirit.

God's weapon is the death of Jesus on the cross, His descent into Hades, His resurrection from the dead on the third day, His ascent into heaven and His constant intercession for all believers today.

God's weapon is that Jesus has *All authority in heaven and on earth...*" (Matt 28:18).

God's weapon is that the Holy Spirit has been poured out and that believers all over the world today have access to God's supernatural presence, knowledge and power.

God's weapon is that Jesus is soon returning and that there one day will be "new heavens and a new earth" when "Christ will be all and in all".

Today we have a tremendous victory through the cross. How much greater will the victory be when eternity steps in, when the kingdom is placed under the lordship of God and the whole earth is filled with His glory. Until that happens, we are to "occupy till he comes".

Ulf Ekman

1

The Church—God's Army

The Bible uses many metaphors for the church. Among other things, the church is spoken of as a temple. A temple has two functions. It is meant for praise and worship and also for intercession. When Jesus cleansed the temple, He said, *"It is written: 'My house shall be called a house of prayer,' but you have made it a 'den of thieves.'"* (Matt 21:13) Just as the temple was a place of prayer and worship, the church of God is that today.

God's church is also likened to a vine. Jesus is the vine and we are the branches. The life, which is in the tree goes out to the branches and these bear fruit. Jesus says, *"He who abides in Me, and I in him, bears much fruit; for without Me you can do nothing."* (Joh 15:5)

Another metaphor of the church is the *body of Christ*. Life flows through the various limbs of it. The limbs are all dependent upon each other and have fellowship with one another. They are also dependent upon Him who is the head of the body, Jesus Christ (Eph 1:22-23; 4:15-16).

Yet another metaphor of the church is the *family of God*. God is our Father and we are His children. The illustration of the believer's relation to God as that of a child emphasizes that you are made righteous before God and that you with boldness can come before His throne. You can just be with Him and know that He loves you and cares for you.

God's Army

There is also the metaphor of the church as *God's army* and it is from this aspect we are going to throw light upon the church and its task. The Holy Spirit emphasizes different things at different times. We need all these metaphors in order to get a complete picture of what the church is, what it is to do and of who God is. One of these metaphors is not enough, but the Holy Spirit stresses different metaphors for different purposes and at different times. He does this so that the need of certain functions in the body of Christ will be able to be met and so that certain tasks will be able to be done.

Now, as we emphasize the metaphor of you and me as soldiers in the army of God, it does not mean that the other functions of the church are not as important. It only means that the Holy Spirit does not always reveal everything all at once, but sometimes focuses on one thing. In recent years, the Holy Spirit has been emphasizing the image of the church as the army of God.

An army makes war. That is its purpose. As soon as one starts talking about war, the devil becomes upset. He does not like it and starts contradicting it, "But Jesus is the Prince of Peace. Don't talk about war so much. Don't use such violent terms. It's repulsive."

When these arguments are presented, it is important to see that the Bible in fact does use war terminology. We do not want to talk of anything other than what God talks of in His Word, but that which the Word talks about, we also want to dare to bring up. Of the metaphors God has given to us as believers, the metaphor of God's army is one which is used the most diligently. In the Old Testament, the people of God, the children of Israel, were continuously engaged in war. This image not only occurs in the Old Testament, but also in the New Testament.

8

The Greater the Importance, the Greater the Opposition

There is no image, no metaphor, subject to fiercer attacks than the image of the church as the army of God. This is because it is so important. If one would, as the devil, want world dominion, one would naturally be very anxious for everybody else to disarm. One would propagate loudly and clearly for disarmament.

If I were at a disadvantage, I would be concerned that those having the advantage would not get an all too great power. If I could get them to disarm, I would catch up with them. That is exactly how spiritual warfare works. If you can get your opponents to scrap their weapons, you automatically have the advantage.

The devil works in this way. If he can lead us believers to believe that we do not have any weapons and that we do not need any either, he will automatically have the advantage. He has been doing this throughout history. His deliberate strategy has been to get God's army to disarm and not use its spiritual weapons. By doing this, he has been able to exercise his destructive influence in a much more powerful way.

Seldom do I meet an opposition stronger than when I preach from Ephesians 6:12. There is nothing the enemy fears more than that we, who are the body of Christ, become conscious of the fact that we are at war. When we realize this, we must behave differently. A soldier lives a completely different life from that of a civilian. If the devil can get you and me to believe that there is peace, when there in fact is a war, he has the chance of defeating us.

We are at War

"For we do not wrestle against flesh and blood, but against principalities, against powers, against the rulers of the darkness of this age, against spiritual hosts of wickedness in the heavenly places" (Eph 6:12).

Now, as we discuss this subject, it is important to realize that we are talking of a spiritual war, not of physical weapons or a physical army. We are talking of the believer as a *spiritual* soldier in a *spiritual* army who make *spiritual* war against a *spiritual* enemy.

Many instinctively react against the word "war". They like "peace" or "serenity" better. Both of these words are derived from the Greek word *"irené"* which means both "outer peace" and "inner peace". We know that God sent His son, so that we would have peace. The question is, then, if it is at all consistent with God, Jesus and Christian faith, to talk about war. Today there are people who claim that it is completely inconsistent. Therefore, we must find out the truth concerning this. Is there a place for spiritual battle in God's character?

"Let them give glory to the Lord, and declare His praise in the coastlands. The Lord shall go forth like a mighty man; He shall stir up His zeal like a man of war. He shall cry out, yes, shout aloud; He shall prevail against His enemies" (Is 42:12-13).

"The Lord is a man of war; the Lord is His name" (Ex 15:3).

In these Bible verses we read that God is a man of war, or a warrior. If God is a warrior, there is room for battle in His character. It says of God that He stirs up His zeal like a man of war and cries out. The small war cries we sometimes make are like the cooing of a baby compared with the cries of the Almighty One. When God whispers, your spirit rumbles. Imagine how it must sound when God gives a war cry!

The Devil's Imitation

Even within the occult there are battle cries. Everything the devil does is an imitation of what God does, has and is. In former days the soldiers stirred up their zeal with the help of the occult, before they went into battle. They would almost go into a trance in order to receive supernatural power and be able to defeat their enemies. Many grotesque things were done so that the soldiers would be rid of their fear and have access to a greater strength than they in fact had.

When the soldiers stirred themselves up, they did so in order to enter into a kind of supernatural concentration. They came into contact with demons. All their strength was concentrated in one direction.

As we all know, the laser beam builds upon this principle. These beams, which as a rule go in a thousand different directions, are focused onto a single spot and thus have a tremendous impact.

God uses the same principle when he stirs Himself up for battle, but He does not need to get strength from anybody else. Nor does He have anything to do with occult powers. Instead, the spiritual life which comes from Him, shatters the influence of occult powers. He takes His own strength and concentrates it in one direction. God involves Himself completely in the battle we are talking about. He stirs up His zeal, He cries out and then the enemy is soon done with.

In the New Testament, we read that Paul in his letter to Timothy encourages him to stir up the gift of God which is in him (2 Tim 1:6). As born-again Christians, we are designed like all the other people in this world, but we have access to another spirit, the Holy Spirit. He eggs you on and stirs up that which God has given you, so that it is not spread out in all directions or is in disfunction. Instead it is brought forth and channeled in one direction. This is what Paul is talking about when he says "stir up". Then he continues, in the same letter, by talking about us being soldiers of Christ (2 Tim 2:3).

No Kingdom of Peace before the Millennium

"For thus the Lord has spoken to me: 'As a lion roars, and a young lion over his prey (when a multitude of shepherds is summoned against him, he will not be afraid of their voice nor be disturbed by their noise), so the Lord of hosts will come down to fight for Mount Zion and for its hill.'" (Is 31:4)

This verse talks of God as a lion and that He will fight as a lion. "Sure," some say, "but this is the Old Testament. When Jesus came, he came bringing peace. He said that it anyone slaps you on your cheek, you should turn the other one to him also." It is correct that Jesus said that. For this reason, we must differentiate between spiritual and physical weapons.

Let us talk about the last thing Jesus will do on this earth. When Jesus returns there will be a thousand years of peace. It will thus be a kingdom of peace which will last a physical millennium.

There are many theories about the biblical Millennium, but the Bible says very clearly that it will be a physical kingdom. Jesus Christ will return in a physical body, resurrected and glorified. In the same way which he was taken up he will come back. In the same place where he was taken up he will return. Just as he physically existed in his resurrective body and had fellowship with the disciples for forty days, before he at a specific point of time in history was physically taken up, he will at another point of time in history physically return in his resurrective body.

When Jesus finally returns, he will come in order to be king of a kingdom which will last a thousand years, a thousand ordinary years. This is a kingdom of peace. When Isaiah 2:4 says that the people shall *"beat their swords into plowshares, and their spears into pruning hooks"*, he is talking about the Millennium. It will be a kingdom of peace, when their will be no physical wars.

Concerning physical wars, Jesus has said that they will keep occurring until he returns.

"And you will hear of wars and rumors of wars. See that you are not troubled; for all these things must come to pass, but the end is not yet. For nation will rise against nation, and kingdom against kingdom. And there will be famines, pestilences, and earthquakes in various places" (Matt 24:6-7).

In the same way, the everyday life will continue until Jesus comes back.

"But as the days of Noah were, so also will the coming of the Son of Man be. For as in the days before the flood, they were eating and drinking, marrying and giving in marriage, until the day that Noah entered the ark, and did not know until the flood came and took them all away, so also will the coming of the Son of Man be" (Matt 24:37-39).

In the age before Jesus returns, there will be people of all professions. People will marry. There will be greed, quarreling over possessions, various types of sensualism and physical wars. The Bible also mentions natural disasters.

Those who believe in and talk of us being able to create a kingdom of peace on earth now do not know what they are talking about. That is nothing but wishful thinking. Only when Jesus returns, will the kingdom of peace be established. There will be a thousand years of peace, during which the glory of God will be manifest of earth like never before. This is the seventh of the seven years. On the seventh day you rest and praise God.

Now, as we are talking of war, it is important to emphasize that we by no means romanticize or glorify war. War is something terrible. It is a result of the Fall of Man and something deeply tragic. It is a suffering beyond description and a gruesome phenomenon.

It is important that you see this in the right context and understand why we are bringing this up. Because we, in this life, are in a spiritual struggle for the soul of Man, and because the Word—especially Paul—uses several military parables, it is natural for us too to do so also. We are simply describing spiritual reality. This is not a game; this is a real, spiritual battle for people's lives to be with or without God. For this reason, the Bible uses illustrations from physical battles in order to explain the battles of the spiritual world for the precious souls of human beings.

The Aim is Peace

What exactly is a war? Well, it is a means of attaining peace. There is no one, not even the cruelest tyrant or dictator, who does not use war as a means of attaining peace. The aim is always peace. This is why any one of those fighting can say that they are lovers of peace. They are—on their own conditions.

The object of acts of war, therefore, is to conquer, expand and overcome, to protect one's own territory and to win over the enemy.

God's purpose is also to conquer, expand and overcome. For this reason, the kingdom of God and that of Satan are at war with each other. That battle will continue until Jesus ends it and establishes the Millennium. This battle is fought all over the world and also in your life. You will not be able to escape it. But, praise the Lord, we are on the winning side. The fight is not between two equal nations. The kingdom of God is infinitely stronger.

It is interesting to see that when Jesus describes the atonement, he describes this too using military terms. On the cross, Jesus conquered, occupied and delivered. In the Gospel of Luke 11:21-22, Jesus says, *"When a strong man, fully armed, guards his own palace, his goods are in peace. But when a stronger than he comes upon him and overcomes him, he takes from him all his armor in which he trusted, and divides his spoils"* (Col 2:15).

In the same way, Paul describes what happened through the death and resurrection of Jesus: *"Having disarmed principalities and powers, He made a public spectacle of them, triumphing over them in it"*.

When you and I read through the Bible, it is revealed to us that there in fact is a war. There is an intense spiritual battle for the life, destiny and future of human beings. Man's life is so precious that when the devil wants to destroy it, God mobilizes everything He has to stop the enemy and to deliver and restore Man. It is small wonder John says in 1 John 3:8: *"For this purpose the Son of God was manifested, that He might destroy the works of the devil"*.

2

The Spiritual Battle

We can read about this war, which we are in the middle of and which this book is about, in the first pages of the Bible.

"Then the Lord God took the man and put him in the garden of Eden to tend and keep it. And the Lord God commanded the man, saying, 'Of every tree of the garden you may freely eat; but of the tree of the knowledge of good and evil you shall not eat, for in the day that you eat of it you shall surely die'" (Gen 2:15-17).

God gave Adam the task and responsibility of taking care of creation, above all the Garden of Eden, to tend to and cultivate and then keep it. The word "keep" means "protect from invaders or theft" and has been translated from the greek word *"shamar"*. Adam's task was, therefore, to take care of and develop this geographical area. He was also to see to it that no one else entered it.

"Keep" can also mean to "fortify" which has to do with the word "fortress" and "defence". Right from the beginning, God tells Adam to maintain a defence. "This is what I have given you," He says. "Make sure you defend it".

God would not have told Adam to protect Eden from invaders if there had not been an enemy. Without an enemy, there would not have been any need of having a defence because there would not have been an outside

threat. But there was an enemy. This enemy was the serpent, Satan, who started out as one of God's arch angels,
but who rebelled against God. He was thrown out of the
presence of God, away from the throne of God. He
became God's enemy and started attacking the image of
God, Man.

The Sly Serpent

What made it possible for the enemy to defeat Adam and
make him fall?

In Genesis 3:1 we read that the serpent was more cunning than any beast of the field. The Hebrew word for
"serpent" also means "whisper" and "shine". You could,
therefore, also say that "the whisperer", "he who shines",
was more cunning than any beast of the field. Then you
see, that this is not a physical snake, but a supernatural
being, which comes in the shape of a physical animal. He
whispers, he shines and he is cunning. That is what your
enemy is like. Whispering, he makes a suggestion. Suggestions that are whispered seldom tolerate coming out into
the light. It is the devil's nature, to come with obscure and
suspicious suggestions.

When it says that the serpent was more cunning than
any beast of the field, this is referring to a supernatural
intelligence, which this serpent possesses. He is sur-
rounded by a form of glory or radiance. But it is not God's
glory, but a result of him being *disguised* as a angel of light.
Light attracts, light gives enlightenment, light gives clarity,
but in this case, the light comes from the wrong source.

Now many believe this was the first time the serpent
came, and that Eve fell at the first try. But it could just as
well have been the hundredth time. That is how the devil
works. To start with, he might have just said, somewhat
discreetly: "I am only passing through. You don't mind me

taking this route, do you?" Because he seemed nice and harmless, they let him make himself more and more at home.

When we read about how the devil finally seduced the woman, we can see what strategy he used, namely to sow distrust against what God had said.

"Now the serpent was more cunning than any beast of the field which the Lord God had made. And he said to the woman, "Has God indeed said, 'You shall not eat of every tree of the garden'?" And the woman said to the serpent, "We may eat of the fruit of the trees of the garden; but of the fruit of the tree which is in the midst of the garden, God has said, 'You shall not eat it, nor shall you touch it, lest you die.'" Then the serpent said to the woman, "You will not surely die. For God knows that in the day you eat of it your eyes will be opened, and you will be like God, knowing good and evil." So when the woman saw that the tree was good for food, that is was pleasant to the eyes, and a tree desirable to make one wise, she took of its fruit and ate. She also gave to her husband with her, and he ate" (Gen 3:1-6).

She gave to her husband, who was with her. If Adam was with her, that means that he stood and watched as everything happened. From the point the serpent started talking, until the point his wife fell, he remained passive and did nothing.

God had told the man, "Protect the Garden against invaders!"

What do you have in your "garden"? Well, you have your family and everything else which belongs to you. Defend them against intruders. It says that the serpent was more cunning than any beast of the field. The serpent was to be on the ground. The ground means not only the physical earth, but the area outside the Garden. That is where the serpent was to stay. Suddenly the serpent entered the Garden—and Adam did nothing.

"So the Lord God said to the serpent: 'Because you have done this, you are cursed more than all cattle, and more than every beast of the field; on your belly you shall go, and you shall eat dust all the days of your life'" (Gen 3:14).

This does not mean that snakes eat dust. But Genesis 2:7 says of Man, that God formed him of the dust of the ground. Then He breathed the breath of life into him. Scientists say that Man and dust consist of some of the same components. This naturally refers to our outer man.

Now God is telling the serpent that he is cursed and that dust will be his food. This means that the devil has the right to eat your "flesh". If you walk according to the flesh, according to your unsaved nature, the devil has the right to take advantage of this against you. Therefore, the Word says,

"Therefore, brethren, we are debtors—not to the flesh, to live according to the flesh. For if you live according to the flesh you will die; but if by the Spirit you put to death the deeds of the body, you will live" (Rom 8:12-13).

War—a Consequence of Adam's Fall

"We know that whoever is born of God does not sin; but he who has been born of God keeps himself, and the wicked one does not touch him" (1 Joh 5:18).

Adam was born of God. Luke 3:38 says that Adam was the son of God. Adam was born of God and if he had kept himself, the devil would not have been able to touch him. If he had kept and protected the Garden against intruders, we would not have had to fight today. All the battles and wars which occur in the world today are the result of Adam's fall.

When Adam fell and the devil got at him, God cursed the serpent and at the same time told it, "You shall eat dust!" What God meant by this was that from now on, new conditions applied, different from those that had applied in the Garden of Eden. Everything in the Garden was lovely as long as the serpent stayed out of it. Our situation today is different in many ways. From the time Man fell, the conditions have been different.

Just before His crucifixion, Jesus told Simon Peter,

"Simon, Simon! Indeed, Satan has asked for you, that he may sift you as wheat. But I have prayed for you, that your faith should not fail; and when you have returned to Me, strengthen your brethren" (Luk 22:31-32).

Jesus knew what would happen when the disciples were tested, but he could also predict what would happen afterwards.

Ever since the fall, all of creation has had to constantly be ready for battle and is in a permanent state of war. The enemy has the right to attack you. Jesus does not say, "No, you cannot touch my sisters and brothers." Nor does God tell him, "You may not touch my children." No, instead Jesus tells us, "I am praying for you, that your faith should not fail". The Bible says that if you keep yourself, the wicked one will not touch you—it does not say that he does not try.

Now For Battle

Most believers have not realized the conditions they live under. For this reason, they are surprised, confused and often disappointed in God when something tragic happens. "Why is this happening to me? What does God mean by this?" they ask themselves.

That is actually like treading around on a mine field and then asking oneself what the explosions are all about. "What is the meaning of this?" There is no meaning at all!

But there is a war, and you did not keep yourself. The enemy got at you.

When we see things as they are and the conditions that apply here on earth, we start acting in a completely different way. We need to learn the rules and play according to them. Then we also see the protection God has given us in the battle, for instance the armor in Ephesians 6.

Some Christians have an intense longing for "peace and quiet", and we will all have peace and quiet—in heaven. Everything will be wonderful there. But down here, it will not be quiet. On the other hand, supernatural help is available, so that you incessantly can win the victory over your enemy, the devil. God has a supernatural peace and joy to give you as you fight, but as long as you are here, you will never have peace, in the sense of absence of battle.

We have not yet reached the point in time where the devil is cast into the bottomless pit and bound for a thousand years (Rev 20:2-3). He progresses from defeat to defeat. He was in heaven but fell down to earth. He had splendor when he was before the throne of God, but he lost it. He has an illusory splendor on earth when he disguises himself as an angel of light.

Something dramatic happened at the cross. The devil lost his power and authority. The next defeat will take place when Jesus returns. Then he will completely lose control over the earth and he will be bound and cast into the bottomless pit for a thousand years. Then he will be released for a short while, so that those who lived in the Millennium will be tested and have the chance to choose for themselves whom they want to serve. After that the devil's influence will definitely be over. He will experience God's consuming glory, in the presence of which no one can stand. He will be cast into the lake of fire and be tormented forever and ever.

Then the war will be over.

You have to know the time you are living in. You cannot act as though you were living in the Millennium now. You cannot act as if there were no enemy. In times of peace you do not need any weapons. Instead, you hang them up on the wall as decorations. But now is not the time to hang up your weapons.

Even though most Christians would never admit it, they have a notion of living in the Millennium now. They behave as if they would not have an enemy. The enemy himself has seen to it that they act in that way. It is his best successful tactic. If he can make you believe you are not subject to attack, or that your friend is the one who is standing against you when it in fact is the devil, he has succeeded with his tactics.

Revival—a Victorious Life

In the light of this, it is interesting to see how upset many become when one speaks of the devil and demons. The Old Testament does not speak much about devil and demons in direct terms. But when Jesus Christ enters the scene, we can read a lot about demonic activity. From the arrival of Jesus to earth until he returns, there is and will be a lot of demonic activity. The presence of the Holy Spirit provokes demonic activity, exposes it and disarms it.

In every revival there has been quite a lot of talk about the devil. But as soon as Christians start backsliding, talk of the devil and his activity is hushed. People being afraid of talking about the devil, is a sign of backsliding. Why? Because revival is actually about a victorious life. It is about an awakening to the fact that the devil is defeated and that we have access to that victory. For this reason, it is very tragic when people are offended by talk of the devil. It is an indication that they have been deceived. We have an enemy and we have to know who he is, so that we can defend ourselves against him.

Naturally, there is sometimes an exaggerated search for the devil and demons, but to completely overlook the believer's enemy, to never mention him or teach what the Bible has to say about him, will only produce an ignorance in spiritual warfare, which will harm the believers.

Going back to Adam and the fall of Man, we can establish that Adam's big mistake was that he took the defence too lightly. Adam did not think he needed a defence. He was careless and did not watch over that which he had been trusted with. He did not take the responsibility God had given him nor use the authority he had received from God.

Adam, as so many others, stood there and just watched it happen. He let himself be led astray, without making the slightest effort at resistance. He laid his weapons down and became a spiritual pacifist. And as a result of this, the entire human race fell into sin. Adam neglected to defend himself. He was more loyal to his wife than to God. For this reason, he lost everything he had, both the glory and the authority.

In a war, the primary aim is not to occupy territory, but to knock out the enemy's weapons. Then you can easily get at his territory. But as long as the enemy still has his weapons, you can never really be sure of victory.

There is a spiritual quality in you which makes you want to guard what you have been entrusted with and see to it that the enemy cannot touch it (1 Tim 6:20). If he has managed to get in, he has to get out. Do not give up until he is out. Refuse to surrender.

Your Own Choice

Adam lost his authority because he refused to fight. For some reason, he did not defend his territory. We do not know why, but maybe he counted the costs and concluded that the price was too high.

Now, as he stands there, listening to Eve speak to the serpent, he notices that she is about to fall. He realizes that if he resists the temptation he will lose her. He listens to the conversation, he hears what the serpent is saying, but he says nothing himself. He sees the serpent offer the fruit, he sees his wife take the fruit and eat of it. When she has taken her first bite of the fruit, he still has a choice, a decision of his own to make. But finally he too eats of the forbidden fruit which is offered to him.

Adam had several opportunities to put a stop to the cunning attacks of the serpent. He was there too. He stood beside Eve the whole time, but he let the enemy be present too.

It Starts with a Thought

Some say, "Where are all these troubles coming from? How could this happen? It came so unexpectedly."

Nothing comes as a surprise. The devil does not just pounce on a person and makes them fall into the gravest of sins. It all starts with a thought. If somebody, for instance, commits adultery, you can be sure that that person had been fooling around with the thought of it for a long time. You can keep up the facade for a time, but sooner or later you succumb to the temptation, which you already have accepted in your thoughts. When the opportunity to sin finally comes, there is no strength to resist it.

On the other hand, if you, every time a wrong thought or temptation comes along, resist it and bring it into captivity to the obedience of Christ, a protection is built up, a strong wall. Then, when the opportunity to sin comes along, the temptation has no power. For this reason, you have to be extremely careful with what you think about. This applies to every area of your life.

When attacks come against a person and he or she falls, others who see this from a distance can become deeply shocked and prove to be utterly unable to understand that such a thing could happen. But there is always a reason why these things happen. The most successful, spirit-filled and powerful preacher does not fall into sin just like that. This only happens when the inner defence is undermined. When the outer pressure increases, the wall crumbles. The devil uses this undermining tactic in all warfare against believers.

Motivation is Essential

If we, as a nation, would get the idea that having a defence is meaningless, with the justification that we would not be able to manage against an attacking nation, we would lay down our defence. When we do this, we fall an easy prey to anybody who wants to conquer us. If you, as an individual soldier get it into your head that it is meaningless or wrong to defend yourself, you will not fight.

The Vietnam War is an example of how a small nation can win over a great nation. At the time, the United States had the most sophisticated and technologically most advanced weapons in the world, but they still were not able to defeat a peasant army. They did not lose because the peasant army was more efficient when it came to physical weapons. Instead, the reason was that this peasant army was extremely efficient when it came to propaganda.

The United States had soldiers with the most advanced weapons but completely lacked the motivation to fight.

They did not know why they were fighting or if it was at all meaningful. They had world opinion against them and were called traitors when they came home on furlough. With soldiers like that, you can be sure of one thing—they will not give everything they've got.

Outward victory calls for inner unity and strength. One cannot have inner conflicts and at the same time have outward victory. For this reason, many occupations of countries begin with revolution. If one can start an inner revolution, the country becomes vulnerable and falls an easy prey to the one who wants to conquer it. Jesus said, *"If a kingdom is divided against itself, that kingdom cannot stand"* (Mark 3:24).

If you do not know that it is worth fighting, if you do not know that there is a victory to be won, you will surrender before you have even begun to fight. If you have been suffering from depression for months or years and do not know that you can get rid of it, you will not take up the fight and win victory over it.

You will not fight unless you have a hope of victory. But if you know that you can be free and if you see that freedom is worth fighting for, you will fight for that freedom and defend yourself in every area in which you are attacked. Then, when you use the weapons God has given, you will have the victory.

Spiritual Intelligence

There are actually three types of war: 1) cold war, 2) conventional war and 3) espionage and subversive activity.

All wars start with espionage. In order to defeat an enemy, you need information about him. You have to know his strong and weak points. You have to find out where the strength in his defence lies and where the weakness is. This calls for espionage.

There is no country on earth that does not exercise some sort of intelligence. On the other hand, there are different types of espionage. There is the general gathering of information, with the purpose of being able to protect one's own territory. There is also a type of espionage in which one enters another country and spies with the aim of conquering that country. Everybody wants information in order to protect themselves and in certain cases to be able to conquer. This goes on all the time in our world and is continually in progress in the spiritual world.

The devil is not almighty. He does not have all knowledge, nor the Holy Spirit. But once, he lived in the presence of God, thus, he has knowledge of God. He knows what it was like to stand before the throne of God. Isaiah 14:12 talks about how he fell and was thrown out of God's heaven.

He builds his tactics upon the knowledge he received a long time ago. In some respects he knows how God thinks. He knows that God does not lie, and he is aware of God being holy and righteous.

The devil knows certain things about God, but he also wants to find out everything about you. For this reason, he has little spies who gather information about you and how you react in different situations. He is a skillful judge of human nature. He has access to very many people and knows very well how Man works.

But when you are born again, you become an inscrutable being to him. As long as you walk in the Spirit, no one can judge you (1 Cor 2:15).

The Battle against the Mind

The deciding factor of every war is not the conventional warfare fought with weapons, but the psychological warfare—the attacks against the minds of the inhabitants. Such infiltration attacks can continue for years. Certain thoughts are planted in people's minds. These thoughts are sown and watered, and finally there is a harvest in the form of an entire system of thoughts, which fits one's own purposes. At this point, people are ready to walk in the wrong direction. This is what happens in wars that are strategically well-planned.

The devil uses the same tactic against you. He plants thoughts in your mind which say, "You are worthless. You are never going to be anybody. There is no victory in your life. Nothing works. You life will always be as it is now. It will not get better. See how you are feeling. Can't you see how insignificant you are?"

You see how you feel and ascertain, "Yes, I am like a grasshopper and my enemies are like giants."

"And they gave the children of Israel a bad report of the land which they had spied out, saying, 'The land through which we have gone as spies is a land that devours its inhabitants, and all the people whom we saw in it are men of great stature. *There we saw the giants (the descendants of Anak came from the giants); and we were like grasshoppers in our own sight, and so we were in their sight*" (Numbers 13:32-33).

Do you know why the children of Israel were not able to enter the promised land? It was not due to insufficient ability, poor weapons or lack of means, strength and power. No, the reason was that the devil defeated them in their minds. He used psychological warfare against them.

He stood before them and said, "We are giants and you are grasshoppers! A grasshopper cannot defeat a giant! It would be better for you to live in the desert that to be beaten here. At least there are oases there. You cannot take this land, for it is a land which devours its inhabitants".

False propaganda! God had said that it was a land flowing of milk and honey (Ex 3:8). The devil said it was a land which devoured its people. Immediately, the spies took the devil's evil report back to the people: "It is a land which devours its inhabitants!"

The devil gradually crumbles the opposition in your mind. All warfare starts with and is won by conquering the mind of the opponent. If you succeed in getting influence over his mind, you can conquer his land. It is for this reason the Bible stresses the importance of protecting one's mind: *"Therefore gird up the loins of your mind, be sober, and rest your hope fully upon the grace that is to be brought to you at the revelation of Jesus Christ"* (1 Pet 1:13).

Make sure you think as God thinks.

Rest in the Battle

Some say, "I am tired of fighting; I want to rest. I want peace and quiet". It is not just important, but absolutely necessary, that you make sure you can rest in the midst of the battle. For you will never get away from the fact that a spiritual battle is constantly in progress.

God has created us in Christ to reign together with Him, and He has given Man authority to reign on earth. If you refuse to take this responsibility, you lose some of your human dignity.

You can choose to be a prisoner. This gives you greater peace and quiet. Many people do make that choice. How much is your freedom worth? That is really what it is all about. Paul says, *"It is for freedom that Christ has set us free"* (Gal 5:1 NIV). The freedom which God through Jesus Christ has given you will constantly be challenged, because Satan is jealous of your freedom. He hates it, because he once had it himself.

No one can be more poisonous and bitter than a backslider. No one can hate God as intensely as he who once knew Him. The devil is backslider number one. Once upon a time, when he stood at the throne of God, he was free. He would love to take the freedom away from you. He will not be set free, but at least he can have some enjoyment by pulling you into the dirt with him. His greatest satisfaction comes from seeing Christians captive, beaten, disappointed and bound. His greatest concern is to try to get you to live in defeat.

No Liberty without Battle

You being able to live in victory automatically means war. When you were born again, you started swimming against the current instead of just floating downstream. There are a thousand opportunities to be popular with everybody and so escape opposition and criticism. All you have to do is change your views now and then. You do not need to say that sickness is from the devil or that God wants to heal all the sick. You can avoid talking about demons, especially religious demons. By simply avoiding the controversial questions, you escape a lot of opposition. But here the question arises once again: How much is freedom worth?

It is all about how highly one values one's freedom. This, in its turn, depends on how much freedom one has. If all you have in your field is three peas, it is easy to think that the Philistines may just as well come and conquer the field. But if you are expecting an abundant harvest in that field, you will make sure you protect it.

If the believers have not been told what they have in Jesus Christ, they will not fight. Only when you have something will you be prepared to fight in order to keep or profit by it. This applies to both the physical and spiritual worlds.

Responsibility and Defence

Man does not readily take on collective responsibility. This is why the collective farms in the former Soviet Union always were so unsuccessful. But in those cases where the peasants had their own little plots, where they could cultivate privately, an interesting observation could be made. There was a considerable difference between the collective fields and the peasant's own patch. If the former looked bare, the latter flourished all the more. The state was something remote and almost undefinable. The further away, the less the worker dedicated himself to the work. But the peasant's patch of land was very near and the dedication became exceedingly greater. God has in fact created us in that way.

This peasant committed himself to his carrots, for they were his own. If they were attacked by vermin, he immediately took care of the problem. He devoted himself more to his own field than to that of the kolkhoz.

We see the same phenomenon when we step into an underground train or a local bus. The person who scribbled all over or ripped the seat covers, would not do that at home. There he feels a different sort of responsibility.

You will defend what you feel responsible for. If you do not have responsibility for anything, you will not have anything to defend either. If you know what you have received, and are thankful for it, you will defend it. If God has given you a Garden, you will protect it, but you choose if you want to do that or not.

This is why faith teaching activates people. Suddenly you start seeing what you have got. When you find out what God has given you as a believer, and then discover that you have not taken part in it, you get moving. You see that something has been stolen from you and you start fighting to get it back.

If you have received something, but do not have it, somebody must have stolen it from you. Who? Well, it could not be God. After all, He was the One Who gave it. When you realize who the thief is, you concentrate all your energy on taking back what rightfully belongs to you through Jesus Christ.

Some people do not understand this. They complain and say, "In the past people confessed their sins. Now all they confess are their rights!" Sure, the word "rights" can be used negatively, when you in a fleshly way demand your rights. But that is certainly not the problem in the body of Christ today. Instead, the problem is that people are being completely mangled by the devil. He tells them that they have nothing, can do nothing nor can ever become anything. He takes their very last ounce of courage and leaves them beaten and low-spirited on the road. This is the greatest problem among Christians today.

When somebody says, "I am righteous in Jesus Christ. I have received the right to be a child of God. God has given me privileges in the new covenant!" the words grate in the ears of religiously-minded people. They think we are behaving as if we were demonstrating for equality or demanding a rise in wages.

That is not at all what we are talking about. We are talking about that which God let Jesus die for to be able to give us. We were the ones who were to have it—not the devil. If we let the devil steal it from us, the purpose will be proven to have been a failure. The purpose of the atonement would prove to be a failure, if we have not taken part in its fruits.

What we are doing is to demand that these rights and privileges, which were given to us through the atonement, be given back to us. We claim them from Satan because he is the one who stole them from us, not from God. God is the one who, because of his omnipotence and love, of His own free will gave them to us.

There are people who have completely misunderstood this and mean that we are threatening God. They think that we stand before God with clenched fists, demanding our rights. That is utterly absurd. The one we are resisting is the devil. It is him we are demanding things of. He is the one who stole from us what God gave to us. There are no reasons whatsoever to make demands on God. He has already given us *everything* through Jesus Christ. It is by His grace we are saved and by His grace we have been blessed.

When we start demanding that Satan return what he stole from us and when we in Jesus' name command the devil to let go of it, the war begins. As long as we accept living on a minimum, things can be calm around us. When we are no longer satisfied with less than constantly living in the spirit and of the spiritual resources, the opposition will be greater than ever.

Due to this, some people give up. They would rather remain in captivity. They want to be spared the opposition but do not realize that they at the same time are losing their freedom. They lose the strength, they lose the joy and eventually they lose the anointing too. Fear enters and rules their lives.

A person who is in captivity is bound. Fear rules that person constantly. If we get this fear into our churches, in the end the result will be us sitting and trying to hush up every sound: "Don't speak too loudly, the devil can hear us." Instead, we are to expose him, so that we can help people get back that which justly belongs to them because of Jesus Christ. In the same way that we can boldly come before God in the name of Jesus and ask for help, we can resist the devil and he *will* flee from us (Jam 4:7).

Motivation to Defend

When I know what belongs to me, I am ready to defend it and fight for it. What we keep coming back to is this: *The most important war is the war of defense.*

What I am talking about now are the principles our actions are based on. If we do not understand these principles we will have unnecessary worries. God wants to spare us these worries. We have a battle to fight, but we do not win that battle by capitulating, deserting or by being spiritual pacifists. Nor do we win it by, as the ostrich, digging our head into the sand and pretending that there is no war. We will never win by fleeing, only by fighting. We have got to reach the point where we see that the fighting is worth it. We have to have that motivation.

The morals of a nation are never higher than its goals. The defence of a nation is not stronger than its motivation to defend itself. This is how it is in the natural and this is true in the spiritual world too. If we are not motivated to fight, we will not pay the price of freedom. For this reason, the Holy Spirit works at making you motivated, so that you do not tolerate just anything. For the same reason, the devil has worked to make us believers as tolerant as possible. There are even principalities who work through ideas such as "mutual understanding" and "tolerance".

Tolerance—but not Compromise

We see each person with respect and we know that God has created and loves that person. We have the ability to be able to make a distinction between person and thing. In that respect we are the most tolerant of all people. We are not aggressive towards anybody, for our fight is not against flesh and blood. But we do not tolerate for one second the demons that destroy people's lives.

I appreciated preacher Dr. Lester Sumrall. He was not afraid of anything. He could walk into and go to sleep in a buddhist temple if he could not find a hotel. He interviewed witch doctors and asked them what they were doing and why. He knew who he was and what he had. He knew that he was free.

That is the freedom we must have. We can spend time with anybody. We are free and know who we are. We walk in ruling, authority, holiness and sanctification, but we will not back to a hair from our convictions.

The aim is not to create a state where everybody believes as we do. That will never happen. But we do want the gospel to be allowed to be preached freely, so that as many as possible hear it and then are able to decide for themselves if they will go to heaven or to hell. We do not want a country where the state determines that the people will go to hell, by preventing them from hearing the gospel. No, there must be freedom, so that each person has a chance to make the choice.

The terrible thing is when people are deprived of the freedom of choice. That is what you and I react against, in the spirit. There must be liberty to hear about and take a stand to Jesus Christ. Not everybody will receive Jesus, but we are working so that as many as possible will. Not everybody will make the right decision. We live side by side with these people. We tolerate and accept them, but we do not tolerate the devil hindering the gospel from being spread.

3

The Warrior

"You therefore must endure hardship as a good soldier of Jesus Christ. No one engaged in warfare entangles himself with the affairs of this life, that he may please him who enlisted him as a soldier. And also if anyone competes in athletics, he is not crowned unless he competes according to the rules. The hardworking farmer must be first to partake of the crops. Consider what I say, and may the Lord give you understanding in all things" (2 Tim 2:3-7).

Here Paul uses three illustrations of the believer: a soldier, an athletic and a farmer. He uses these illustrations to show you what being a Christian is like. All three have one thing in common—they *do* something. It is one of the conditions of the spiritual life, that you and I do something.

All three also *receive* something, as a result of sweat and labor. The soldier conquers, the athletic wins and the farmer bears fruit. None of these get results without having made an effort.

Faith Works

Sometimes people say: "Faith is not an achievement; it is resting in God's achievement!" That sounds very nice and it is true, but it is not the whole truth. People usually say that when the work starts getting sweaty.

Now of course there are those who misunderstand faith teaching and turn it into something desperate. They think it is all about achievement, in the sense that one has to earn something through works. Faith is not a desperate achievement, but it still involves work. Faith without works is dead, as we read in James 2:26.

Faith acts. Based on the faith of your heart, you do something. What do you do? You fight, you compete and you plow. You are a soldier, an athlete and a farmer. If you do not want to accept this fact, you will not have any results. You have to know and adapt yourself according to the terms which apply.

For this reason, Paul says when he draws a parallel between the believer and the warrior, *"You therefore must endure hardship as a good soldier of Jesus Christ"*. Some other translations read: "endure suffering"

A soldier's life does not consist of sitting in camp, polishing his uniform buttons. Nor is his task to parade down the street, showing off his uniform. He is meant to lie in a trench, fight and occupy territory. This is a job. This is what we, step by step, are learning to do. We are trained to work and live under pressure, so that we are constantly well-prepared and will not be knocked out in the first round.

You Are Always a Soldier

Many believers do not understand the spiritual battle in meetings. They have their own ideas of what a meeting is—the anointing flows and they sit and lap up the cream— everything is served and ready for them.

When opposition and irritation, control, sleepiness then arise, and when sluggishness and downheartedness begin to be manifest, many give up. They spend the rest of the meeting wondering why it is not as free in this meeting as in the other meetings.

The problem is that many attend meetings in order to relax. When you do that, you sit disarmed, and the devil immediately takes advantage of your passivity. It gives him the opportunity to enter with dejection, confusion and rebellion. After a few minutes you are sunk and you sit there wondering what really happened. Then it can take a while before you win back what you lost and you have to concentrate all the power which has been put at your disposal, in order to strike back against the devil.

What we are striving for, and what God is teaching us, is not to fight so that we only just get by. We want to get the devil completely out of the way, disarmed and driven off. Then God can do so much more and take us much further and higher up.

It is one thing to fight to occupy yet another meter and dig a new trench there. It is something completely different to occupy an entire territory at once and then keep it. This is what the Holy Spirit is teaching us.

The first step is to know that you always are a soldier: *"Endure hardship as a good soldier of Jesus Christ."* You are always a soldier. You are always in service and there will always be attacks. This is normal. So when you feel as if you are backsliding and God seems far away, this is because you feel the war which is going on in the spiritual world. If you take up the fight against the devil you have to count on him counterattacking.

Therefore, do not believe every emotion or thought which comes against you. Be aware that you are at war. Learn from every attack, to be watchful and alert, so that your enemy cannot get at you from any ambush the next time he attacks. Instead, you do battle against him and make him flee. You endure your hardship as a soldier of

Jesus. You fight the good fight. You know why you are fighting. You become used to enduring hardships. You learn to work under pressure, for you know that the result is worth all the pain.

When I experience this type of pressure and opposition I know that something is about to happen. When the devil is aggressive, I know that he is nervous. If I stand firm and continue, there will be a breakthrough. If the devil was not afraid and did not feel threatened, he would never take the pains of making such attacks. He leaves the dead alone; they cannot resist him. It is the life he wants to choke. But we refuse to let him do that. The Gospel of John 1:5 says, *"The light shines through the darkness, and the darkness can never extinguish it"* (New Living Translation). The devil can not put out that light.

If we continue without getting weary or giving up, the devil backs off. If you back when there is pressure in your life, he will know it. He will know how you react. He will know how much you can take and he will know when you give up. So the next time you witness, preach, pray for people, whatever you do, he will know where your weak point is. He will know that you give up if you do not see results immediately. So he will hold on five minutes longer than you are willing to hold on. But if he knows that you *never* give up, he has to give in.

Never Give Up!

Your enemy, the devil, does not have all power nor does he have all knowledge. He obtains information by watching you. He acquires knowledge about you by sowing a thought in your head and then seeing how you react to that thought. If you are undisciplined and have not girded up the loins of your mind, what is most probable is that that thought immediately comes out of your mouth.

The devil whispers, "You are tired now, it is time to go home!" Immediately you say, "I am tired now, it is time to go home!" And you are defeated. Often the victory lies only a few minutes ahead. A soldier has perseverance and patience. That is where the victory lies.

The devil says, "This is what the rest of your life is going to be like. You might as well give up!" Then you have got to say, "No, it will not be like this for much longer. So I will not give up. Even if it would continue for a thousand years, I will never give up. I have made up my mind never to give up. But because I never give up, it will not continue for a thousand years; it will only last a short while! I have received it in faith and that is how it will be."

"Therefore I tell you, whatever you ask for in prayer, believe that you have received it, and it will be yours" (Mark 11:24 NIV). There is a time span between *"have"* and *"will be"*. The more convinced you are that you "have received" it, the shorter the distance will be to it "will be yours". For this reason, you should refuse to back. On the contrary, you recognize the resistance, know that you have chosen to fight, and enjoy yet another victory.

I once asked the Lord how long I would have to keep fighting, standing in faith for things and resisting the devil. The Lord answered me and said, "Your days on earth are like the days of a warrior". Later I discovered that there is a similar Bible verse in the book of Job 7:1, *"Is there not a time of service for man on earth?"*

As long as you want victory, there will be a fight. As long as there is a fight, you have to make sure you are a warrior. As long as you are a warrior, there is victory, because you have weapons and you can win every battle.

In Joel 2 the Bible says that there in the end time will be an entire generation of "soldiers". Soldiers have always existed, but there has never been an entire generation of them. This is why the teaching on faith must be proclaimed. Faith is what will give people victory and chase the devil out of cities, districts, counties, regions and countries.

Fight According to the Rules!

The soldier, the athlete and the farmer all fight a battle. The athlete has one thing in sight, and that is to win. But he will not win if he does not compete according to the rules (2 Tim 2:5). First Corinthians 9:24 says, *"Run in such a way as to get the prize"* (NIV).

We are not in the battle only to participate; we are in the battle to win. We only have one purpose and that is to win the battle. The Bible, however, says that we cannot win unless we fight according to the rules. For there are rules to fight, compete and work according to. When you know which rules apply, you can win.

If God has given you rules on how to win, it will not help to merely cry to God, "Do something!". You will not win unless you follow the rules. When you do, you will win every time you do battle. When the Bible says "battle", it means that you have to do something. When it says "weapons" it means that you use them. When it says "run" it means that you are to run. Only when you do this, will something happen.

A lot of counselling and tragedies in people's lives could have been avoided if those concerned had known of the necessity to fight. But the church has failed when it comes to teaching about this subject from the Word of God. For this reason, the devil has been able to strike thousands of people, who now lie beaten and have to be counselled and helped for years, before they can get back on their feet again. They would have been restored a long time ago if they had known which rules to run according to. We have all been deceived, but when we finally do discover the truth, the devil will no longer be able to get the better of us.

"Blessed shall you be when you come in, and blessed shall you be when you go out. The Lord will cause your enemies who rise against you to be defeated before your face; they shall come out against you one way and flee before you seven ways" (Deut 28:6-7).

This is a promise from God to the people of Israel, God's army. If one transfers that to the conditions of the new covenant, this promise applies to the spiritual battle which we are in. Then the enemies are no longer Philistines, Ammonites or Moabites, but principalities, powers and rulers of darkness. When these, your enemies, rise up against you, the Lord will cause them to be defeated before you. They will come out against you one way but flee before you seven ways. This is a tremendous promise from the Lord, which says that you can live in victory over your enemies.

Irrational Resistance

"Then all peoples of the earth shall see that you are called by the name of the Lord, and they shall be afraid of you" (Deut 28:10).

The peoples of the Old Testament were never favorably disposed toward the children of Israel. In the same way the world is not kindly disposed to you as a believer. We are not first of all talking about people in the world, but about the principalities which are ruling in the world. If they are kindly disposed towards you, something is wrong with you. Then you have lost your flavor.

Jesus said: *"Woe to you when all men speak well of you!"* (Luk 6:26) This verse does not mean that people can never speak well of us, individually and personally. But if the world as a whole and non-Christians in general think we are wonderful, then something is seriously wrong. Then we have slipped over to their side.

If you follow the Lord and walk in His blessings, some people will harbor a kind of fear for you. They can have an almost unmotivated fear or respect, which also can verge on hatred. You are strange in their eyes and they don't quite know how to treat you. Make sure, then, that they think you are peculiar for good reasons, not because you do crazy things!

"If you are insulted because of the name of Christ, you are blessed, for the spirit of glory and of God rests on you. If you suffer, it should not be as a murderer or thief or any other kind of criminal, or even as a meddler. However, if you suffer as a Christian, do not be ashamed, but praise God that you bear that name" (1 Pet 4:14-16 NIV).

The people of God are always different in the eyes of the world. They do not always understand why they react as they do to the people of God, and why decisions sometimes are made on totally irrational grounds.

A few years ago, for instance, I watched a debate on television about the persecution of Jews in the Soviet Union. One of those taking part said that he could not understand this persecution. He thought it was so irrational. There was no logical reason at all why just that people group should be persecuted. No one who participated in the discussion could answer the question why the Jews of all people were the ones being persecuted in the Soviet Union.

He who does not have the Biblical revelation on this does not understand it. Even if it is completely irrational from a natural perspective, it is not at all so from a spiritual one. The Jews are still God's peculiar people. This does not mean that they are born again, but they are God's people and God's tools in this world. And they will remain so until Jesus Christ returns.

When Haman in the book of Esther wanted to kill all the Jews, he did not know the real reason why he hated them. He hated Mordecai, because he refused to bow before him. He was jealous of Mordecai, and for this reason, he wanted to kill everybody who was related to him. He wanted to kill an entire people because one man would not bow down. This was completely illogical and irrational. But in the spirit world it was a very deliberate move. It was only one of many ways of trying to kill off God's people and in this way prevent the Messiah from coming.

Fear—Your Worst Enemy

If your enemy has fear, see to it that you yourself do not have fear. The harlot Rahab is a good example of this. When the two spies came to her, she said,

"I know that the Lord has given you the land, that the terror of you has fallen on us, and that all the inhabitants of the land are fainthearted because of you. For we have heard how the Lord dried up the water of the Red Sea for you when you came out of Egypt, and what you did to the two kings of the Amorites who were on the other side of the Jordan, Sihon and Og, whom you utterly destroyed. And as soon as we heard these things, our hearts melted; neither did there remain any more courage in anyone because of you, for the Lord your God, He is God in heaven above and on earth below" (Jos 2:9-11).

The inhabitants of Jericho had been afraid for forty years. At the same time, the children of Israel had spent all these years in the desert, also afraid. They said, "This land is full of giants; we cannot conquer it." But in the land the "giants" were terrified that the children of Israel would come upon them. Both peoples were afraid, each on their own side.

In war, there is nothing more destructive than fear. The American president Franklin D. Roosevelt introduced the following phrase during the Great Depression in the 1930s: "We have nothing to fear but fear itself." Nothing can break down defence, resistance, power of initiative and offensiveness as effectively as fear. Fear is our worst enemy.

If we have the victory over fear, we automatically have the victory over everything else, too. Our projects and everything we set about to do, do not constitute a problem when we are free from fear. Then everything moves along automatically.

I noticed this very clearly when we built our new building for Word of Life. Nothing has been so easy to have faith for as this. During the whole time of building. I was not once afraid that it would not be completed because God had given me an assurance about it.

When God gives you something, fear disappears. Only when God's plans and ideas are planted in your heart, in your spirit, does fear disappear. As long as you do not have it in your spirit, but only in your thoughts, in your soul, the fear will remain. Fear makes you a lousy soldier.

Young David proved this when he entered the camp where Saul and all the soldiers were paralysed with fear for Goliath (1 Sam 17). The entire army of Israel was overcome by fear, even though God had said, *"The Lord will cause your enemies who rise against you to be defeated before your face"* (Deut 28:7). Fear can conquer an entire army.

The Lord's Fight Through You

There is a problem here, and that is the interpretation of how the battle is to be done. Some believe that victory is won in a jiffy. But when the Bible talks of "our struggle", it is speaking of a fight which is like a wrestling match. It is a long, drawn-out fight, not something which can be settled with a single blow.

Because it says, *"The Lord will cause them to be defeated"*, some think the Lord will fight in their place, but that is wrong. The Lord does not fight *in your place*, He does it *through* you. This principle recurs in everything. The Lord does not do it *instead* of you; He does it *through* you.

So do not pray to God that He fight for you, so that you can lie at home, sleeping. On the other hand, you can pray, "God, you take care of this," in the knowledge that you cannot do anything in yourself. This principle is found throughout the Old Testament: the people cry out and pray to God, and then go out and crush the enemy. After this is done they say that the Lord defeated the enemy for them.

There are examples of when the people did not fight. One such occasion is described in 2 Chronicles 20:17. But in that case they still did exactly what the Lord said at that time. They obeyed the instructions they were given, and these varied from time to time. But in most cases we can see that angels did not descend from heaven to defeat the enemy in their place. It sometimes happened that such confusion broke out among the enemies that they started to fight each other, but this is not the usual course.

On another occasion Joshua commanded the sun to stand still (Jos 10:12). One could think that he, if he had been smart, could have asked God to send 10 000 angels to destroy the enemy all at once, so that they themselves would be able to take it a bit easy. But he did not do that. He said, *"'Sun, stand still over Gibeon; and Moon, in the Valley of Aijalon.' So the sun stood still, and the moon stopped, till the people had revenge upon their enemies"* (Jos 10:12-13).

One could ask the same of Moses. Why didn't Moses pray to God, that He would let hail and fire fall over the

Amalekites when these attacked Israel? Instead he held up his hands before God. As long as Moses held up his hands, Israel prevailed over the Amalekites. When he let his hands down, the Amalekites prevailed over the Israelites.

This is the principle of the walk of faith and the authority of the believer. We walk with the Lord and he works through us. If we do nothing, nothing gets done.

Guaranteed Victory—If you Fight

Nothing will get done before you decide to act. If you, for example are sick, you can cry out to God both day and night without getting well, but when you let your faith be manifested in action, something happens. The moment you say, "No, that is enough!", the power of God comes.

You will not have victory before you make up your mind, pick up your weapons and go to attack—attack against lack, poverty, sickness, depression, self-pity or whatever it is you need victory over. The opposition will not vanish before you attack. When you attack, it has to retreat before you. If the opposition has come against you on one way, it has to flee from you on seven ways.

The promise God has given us soldiers is that each one of us can chase a thousand and that two can chase ten thousand (Deut 32:30). We are to chase them and they will flee. This means that we have a guaranteed victory, in every battle, in our struggle. We have been promised victory in every battle. This makes it all the more fun. But if the devil can get you to believe that you will not win, or if you fear losing, you will not have the victory.

This is where things went wrong for the Israelite army. Each individual soldier had been promised victory, but none of them took it to themselves. Each individual soldier would have been able to put Goliath to flight, based on the promise that one chases a thousand and two put ten thousand to flight.

Jonathan proved this when he took his armorbearer with him and went out to defeat the Philistines. He said, *"Come, let us go over to the garrison of these uncircumcised; it may be that the Lord will work for us. For nothing restrains the Lord from saving by many or by few"* (1 Sam 14:6). And so they climbed up the hill and cleared it of Philistines, even though there were only two of them.

God had promised victory. In Joshua 1:3 God says to the children of Israel that He has given them the land, *"Every place that the sole of your foot will tread upon I have given you..."*. You have a delightful advantage when you enter a land and know that you will be given every place your foot treads upon. The only thing you need to do to get a place is to tread upon it. That does not mean that it *feels* as if you will receive it, or that you understand how it will happen. It means nothing more than that God has said *that you will* be given it.

A Personal War

"Now these are the nations which the Lord left, that He might test Israel by them, that is, all who had not known any of the wars in Canaan (this was only so that the generations of the children of Israel might be taught to know war, at least those who had not formerly known it)..." (Judges 3:1-2).

What is God doing here? He is allowing some foreign peoples to remain in the promised land. Why? So that the grandchildren of Israel, that is the generation which grew up in the promised land, also would learn to defeat their enemies.

War is personal. I have a personal war against the devil, and so do you. You can not fight my battle and I cannot fight yours, but we fight together.

If you live close to me, as I fight my personal battle, and you do not care about your own personal battle, you will not learn to fight. You will not learn to fight by seeing me fight. You only learn to fight by fighting yourself. You can listen to my tapes, read my books, listen to others' tapes, read their books, hear their stories and become so happy, but still never learn to do battle.

You can never learn to fight without entering the fight yourself. This is why God let some of the foreign people remain in the land, to teach the descendants of the children of Israel how to make war. God taught them to fight by letting them take part in the battle.

When you are attacked in life, do not be ashamed of this. Do not run away from the attacks or make excuses for them. Your being attacked does not mean that you are a backslider. If you run from the attacks, you will never have the victory over them. Instead, declare war on them.

Thorns—Supernatural Opposition

John Wesley had a wife who hated everything he did. Sometimes, when he returned from his most successful campaigns, she would lock him out of the house. He had his own personal war. All men of God, throughout history, have had wars. The devil suspected from the very beginning what was to become of them and therefore tried to break them.

The devil anticipates what can become of you. He hopes that you will never be anything for God and that you never will respond to God's calling. But he cannot be sure of this and for this reason, he makes long-term plans. He uses the spirit of this world, your own flesh and his own demons. He has strategically placed demons, whose aim is to prevent you from becoming what God has planned for you.

Paul was attacked in many areas of his life. One of these afflictions, he called a thorn (2 Cor 12:7). A principality, a messenger of Satan, was posted against him. If you have a ministry, you will now and then and in certain places be met with particular resistance.

In the Old Testament we see the explanation for what a thorn is:

"But if you do not drive out the inhabitants of the land from before you, then it shall be that those whom you let remain shall be irritants in your eyes and thorns in your sides, and they shall harass you in the land where you dwell." Num 33:55

"...know for certain that the Lord your God will no longer drive out these nations from before you. But they shall be snares and traps to you, and scourges on your sides and thorns in your eyes, until you perish from this good land which the Lord your God has given you." Jos 23:13

Israel's thorn was the foreign people. In 2 Corinthians 12:7, Paul writes, *"And lest I should be exalted above measure by the abundance of the revelations, a thorn in the flesh was given to me, a messenger of Satan to buffet me, lest I be exalted above measure"*. An annotation to this verse in a Swedish Bible translation gives the following explanation of the word "thorn": "It is unknown what Paul is referring to. Some have guessed various diseases. As the word in the original text in the Septuagint is used of the enemies of Israel (Numbers 33:55, Ez 28:24), it is more probable that he is thinking of a difficult opponent."

A thorn is supernatural, demonic resistance which comes against you because you are a servant of the Lord.

Martin Luther translated the New Testament from Greek to German in three months. He was both excommunicated and outlawed and sat in a tower, translating. Whoever wanted to could kill him. He was in a hurry, for he did not know when they would find him. He was tremendously harassed.

A tribulation is a conscious attack from the devil in order to render your ministry harmless. If you are serving God such attacks will come. There are a great number of different kinds of attacks. Fundamental attacks are pride and temptations in such areas as sex and money. But what we are talking about here are other attacks, attacks which come through those nearest to you, your family or your co-workers. They came against Jesus through Judas. They came against Paul through Demas. An undercurrent of opposition and subversive activity constantly followed in their footsteps.

Jesus was together with Judas for three and a half years. He knew all the time that Judas one day would publicly betray him and lie about him. In spite of this, He gave Judas the responsibility of being treasurer. The spirit which worked in Judas constantly struck against Jesus. Peter and the other disciples were sometimes under the wrong influence, but their hearts were right. Judas was different.

Live with Goals

That which is in a person's heart comes out when she or he speaks. *"For out of the abundance of the heart the mouth speaks"* (Matt 12:34). Listen to what the mouth says and you will know what is going on in the heart.

When God does something it is visible and the Bible talks of tangible results of God's actions. You are not to look at your neighbor and compare yourself with him. But know that God wants to give you results and fruits that are visible.

The main objective of our commander-in-chief Jesus Christ is the Great Commandment. In an ordinary war, the commander-in-chief gives orders of what each person is to do. The main objective is divided into smaller, clear objectives, which suit the individual soldier. Everybody knows what they are to do.

Even if Jesus said that we are to go into all the world, you know that you cannot immediately go into all the world. The overall objective has to be divided into smaller constituents so that each person knows what to do for the moment. If you learn to live with the correct aims, your life will be successful.

Most people do not live according to goals but according to activities and problems. Most of us have grown up in a generation which thinks no longer than till Saturday. Our entire lives are centered around experiences: "Is there something good on TV?" We has to feel or experience something—go to the movies or go out to dance.

If you do not let the Holy Spirit bring you out of this experience-centered lifestyle, you will be beaten time after time. You will not be able to experience what you are dreaming of, but rather the opposite.

You have to become disciplined and goal-orientated in everything you do, and learn to see beyond your nose. You need to think years ahead. The victories you will have in a few years' time will be owing to your preparing for them now and putting your life into alignment with them. Do not let your life be steered by problems and activities, but let your life be directed by goals. God wants to give you clear goals which you can work towards.

There are long-range goals which last throughout your life. You may have received a Bible verse, which lasts a for your entire lifetime. I received one such "life verse" from the Lord in 1970. It is Psalm 27:4: *"One thing I have desired of the Lord, that will I seek: that I may dwell in the house of the Lord all the days of my life, to behold the beauty of the Lord, and to inquire in His temple"*. This is what I, more than anything else, want for my life. Everything I do is a result of this.

Ask God for a word for the rest of your life. Make sure you get a clear direction for your life. Then God will give you more detailed instructions. If you do what you are supposed to do now, God will entrust you with more. When He speaks to you, write down what He says, and aim your life according to it. Remain in what God has said. Do not look in other directions. What God has said is all that matters.

Our lives follow a carefully organized plan. God knows what He is doing. Not one experience in your life is in vain. The evil which the devil plans for you, God turns to something good. God takes the most terrible experiences in your life and makes something good of them, if you recognize what God has told you. God can put thoughts and plans in you, which you might not understand until twenty or thirty years later. Plan for a long life on earth, even if Jesus would come tomorrow. Work purposefully under the guidance of the Holy Spirit and let Him correct your plans.

4

Principles for Victorious Warfare

In order to be victorious in battle you need to follow the basic principles of warfare. In this chapter I will discuss ten principles. Before I go through them, however, I want to talk a little about the function of an army.

An army is well-equipped. An army is fit for battle. An army has precise divisions in different combatant units. In an army every soldier knows his function and place. In an army there is a strict order of precedence. In an army everybody has a common goal and an inner unity. In an army there is a measure of discipline which is greater than in civil life, because the tasks demand it. All of this is in an army.

If this does not exist in God's army, disorder, chaos and defeat will come instead. When teaching on these functions is not stressed, the believers become slack, apathetic, problem-centered and weak, and thus fall an easy prey to the enemy. For this reason, the task to equip and train the army of God is extremely important today and therefore the opposition against this is also great.

Paul says in Colossians 2:5,

"For though I am absent from you in body, I am present with you in spirit and delight to see how orderly you are and how firm your faith in Christ is." (NIV)

The word "order" can be translated to mean "exact, military order". God is, in other words, happy when there is firmness and order in His army because then it can overcome the enemy much more easily.

1. The Principle of Objectives

The first principle in winning a war is to be absolutely clear in one's objective. As a servant of the Lord you need peace and security. You can experience it when you know that you are following the plan of God. Do not shoot at random, test everything first. Follow the plans God has shown you. That which you are doing now, do it whole-heartedly and He will reveal more to you as time goes by.

A war is won by the objective being clearly conveyed to the soldiers—or, if we translate it into the spiritual terms— to those working for a vision. One example of an all-embracing goal can be the Great Commission in the Gospel of Matthew 28:18-20.

In Colossians 1:28-29 we find Paul's objective:

We proclaim him, admonishing and teaching everyone with all wisdom, so that we may present everyone perfect in Christ. To this end I labor, struggling with all his energy, which so powerfully works in me. (NIV)

2. The Principle of an Offensive Spirit

The second principle is having an offensive spirit. A war can never be won through passivity; you have to be on the offensive. Attack is the best defence. This has been the case in all wars. You have time to go to attack before the enemy attacks and he has to instead concentrate (his strength) on defending himself. If I have an enemy and know that he sooner or later is going to attack me, the best thing is if I attack him first. This is how wars are won.

The Israelis won the Six Day War in 1967 because they knew that the countries surrounding Israel were starting to mobilize against them. President Nasser in Egypt urged 50 million arabs to go to attack. At first Israel waited for them to attack but finally made the decision not to wait any longer. Israel knew that it would not be long before the Arabs would be upon them. They decided to attack first, since Egypt already had launched acts of war by blocking the Strait of Tiran. They used their most powerful weapon, the air force, and knocked out the entire Egyptian air force—on the ground. While the Egyptian soldiers sat in their planes waiting for orders, the Israeli soldiers came and crushed their air force completely.

In a war where one knows that a mobilization is in order, attack is the best defence. The same applies on the spiritual level. When there is about to be an attack of some sort, for instance a cold, we often feel it coming in advance. We notice when the symptoms start looming large before the cold breaks out. In spite of this we sometimes end up in bed for a week or more. Why? We neglected to attack and the enemy had time to attack us first. We could have had the upper hand and stopped that which came against us, which did not have as great power in the beginning. But instead, we became the underdog and had to fight our way up from there.

3. The Principle of Goals

In war one cannot simply wildly strike at everything. In order to be able to win a war you have to strike at the right point. Sure, you can gather an entire army, march into the desert, shoot at sanddunes and think you've achieved very much indeed. To be sure you would use up a lot of ammunition, but you will not win any wars in that way. Many times this is exactly what we do, when we pray and fight in the spirit or hold campaigns that have been less carefully planned.

In all military strategy there is a decisive point, a place for breakthrough. The aim of battle is the break through the lines of the enemy and make him retreat. It is a fact that our enemy, the devil, also has a line of defence, just as we do, and you can conquer it. There are weaker and stronger points on that line and we will break through on his weakest point. The devil's weakest point is love! He does not have any weapon against it. For this reason it says, *"For God so loved the world that he gave his one and only Son..."* (Joh 3:16 NIV). That is what the decisive battle was about.

The final battle has already taken place where our enemy the devil is concerned. Jesus fought the decisive battle on Calvary, a battle which meant a complete breakthrough and disarming of our enemy's army. What we are doing today, using military terminology, is purging. We are proclaiming in area after area that the capitulation already has taken place. The surrender took place on Calvary two thousand years ago, and now we are entering region after region, telling the enemy, "You are already defeated. You might as well give up and get out of here. The victory is already won." Historically, the decisive battle has already taken place. This applies also to your personal life.

It is important to understand this, because many waste a lot of gunpowder and a lot of energy on the wrong things. If the devil can get us to fight in the wrong arenas, he will make us lose our concentration in those arenas where we really should take up the fight.

We fight about baptism, we fight about the communion, we fight about church rules and regulations, fight about this and that. We make war according to the rules, but we fight it first of all with the wrong means, because we are fighting in the flesh, and secondly in the wrong place, on the wrong side of the line of defence. Our enemy the devil is the one who lies behind these doctrinal arguments, in which we shoot at each other instead of at our enemy. You have to decide if that which you are fighting about really is worth fighting for. Are you in the real war or are you only shooting at barrages?

During World War Two the allies had planes in the air from which they threw tons of tinfoil over the English Channel and Holland. These dots looked like airplanes on the German radar screens. They thought a mighty squadron was coming against them, but in reality all it was, was tinfoil!

This is exactly what the devil does. He uses some bitter person who has not been allowed to make a shining appearance, who has not been allowed to show off his talents and who now sits at home, full of disappointment. If you look at the doctrinal arguments which have been fought throughout history you can see that they often are initiated by such people. Their motives are not pure, and they are not on the front line, fighting. It is important that you are aware of this and decide what is worth fighting. Do not shoot at everything that moves, but save your energy until you reach the point where there can be a breakthrough. Where is it? Where is the devil's sensitive spot? Where is his weakness? That is where you make your thrust.

Jesus knew exactly what to do to get the devil to lay bare his weak point, and the disciples did too. When the lame man in Acts 3 was healed, the authority in the name of Jesus resulted in the Council wanting to put them in jail. The elders asked them, *"By what power or what name did you do this?"* (Acts 4:7 NIV). Then Peter answered, *"It is by the name of Jesus Christ of Nazareth... that this man stands before you healed."* (Acts 4:10 NIV). Then we see that they went home and prayed that God in an even more powerful way would heal the sick through the name of His holy servant Jesus. They received information about what was important by observing where the greatest reactions of resistance were. That is where there was a point of breakthrough.

4. The Principle of Concentration

The key to success in what you do lies in your ability to concentrate—physically, mentally and spiritually. People today have a hard time concentrating. They are swamped with impressions from every direction—television, newspapers and much more. The devil's purpose with this is to destroy people's ability to concentrate. For Man's power and strength lie in his ability to concentrate.

Even in praying for people it is necessary to be concentrated on what you are doing, because if you are not you cannot deliver anything. It is not enough to lay hands on people; by spiritual concentration you must take what you have and give it to the people you are praying for.

The ability to concentrate is significant in many respects. The strength of the first church was that the believers were focused on the Word, prayer, the teaching of the apostles and signs and wonders.

This is why Jesus says in the Gospel of Matthew 18:19, *"Again I say to you that if two of you agree on earth concerning anything that they ask, it will be done for them by My Father in heaven"*. This means to be in one accord, to concentrate together with ones partner. With that concentration comes an ability to shut out other impulses. The energy goes in one single direction. You become like a she-bear who sees that her young ones are in danger. She is completely concentrated on one thing only—to defend her young. With this type of concentration, the victory will be yours. The victory may not become reality immediately, but the decisive battle will take place where you break through.

One basic principle in war is that the strongest one wins. If an inferior force beats a superior one, this is due to the principle of concentration. An inferior force can concentrate a greater force on a decisive point at a certain time and thus win the battle.

This is what happened with Gideon. He struck down tens of thousands, maybe even hundreds of thousands of soldiers with three hundred men (Judg 7). This dealt with the principle of concentration. To start with they were considerably more in number, but many lacked courage and therefore had to turn home.

"And the Lord said to Gideon, "The people who are with you are too many for Me to give the Midianites into their hands, lest Israel claim glory for itself against Me, saying, 'My own hand has saved me.' Now therefore, proclaim in the hearing of the people, saying, 'Whoever is fearful and afraid, let him turn and depart at once from Mount Gilead.'" And twenty-two thousand of the people returned, and ten thousand remained. But the Lord said to Gideon, "The people are still too many; bring them down to the water, and I will test them for you there. Then it will be, that of whom I say to you, 'This one shall go with you,' the same shall go with you; and of whomever I say to you, 'This one shall not go with you,' the same shall not go." So he brought the people down to the water. And the Lord said to Gideon, "Everyone who laps from the water with his tongue, as a dog laps, you shall set apart by himself; likewise everyone who gets down on his knees to drink." And the number of those who lapped, putting their hand to their mouth, was three hundred men; but all the rest of the people got down on their knees to drink water." (Judg 7:2-6)

Spiritual power is not always released through a physically superior number of people; it has to do with the attitude of the heart. God reduced the troop to three hundred men— three hundred men who were fearless, concentrated and who whole-heartedly released more power than that which the entire great force of the enemy could do. With these men, the enemy could be defeated, and Gideon's men won the battle in spite of their inferiority. Concentration releases unusual strength.

5. The Principle of Flexibility

In Exodus 12:51 we read about an entire people being moved in a single day. The entire people of Israel, several million people, pulled out of Egypt on the same day. That's movability for you! It was a miracle that everybody left Egypt and that nobody remained behind. Abraham in his day left his country even though he did not know where he would end up. The principle of flexibility is absolutely necessary in winning a war. In God's eyes David was a capable soldier. That which more than anything else characterized David was his ability to be flexible.

The principle of flexibility involves being quicker, more flexible, more efficient and movable than the enemy. You can only be these things if you are trained and committed, and you will not become those things without some effort.

Saul's house became weaker and weaker, while David's became stronger and stronger. Eventually, David became king over all of Israel. In the midst of all the battle and flight which constantly was a part of David's life, he learned to put his trust in God. He also learned never to take a victory for granted and never to repeat a manner of attack, but always to take direct orders from God in the situation he was in (2 Sam 5:19-25). David never did the same thing twice. He always asked God what to do first and he never got the same answer.

You cannot rely on one method. You have to listen to what God says specifically on each occasion. God knows where the enemy is at, what his strength is and what his weakness is. God knows the situation precisely, and tells you which initiatives you need to take. At this point, you have to be flexible. One sign that revival has disappeared is that the flexibility and agility have also disappeared. Everybody does things the way they have always done them.

It is possible to retain the flexibility and thereby continue walking with God. When we do that, the devil will not be able to reach us. The devil studies you and forms for himself a picture of what you are like. When you later do something unexpected, he has to form a new picture of you. The enemy loses control over you when you are flexible. You always get through to the other side, and he cannot reach you.

Conservatism and traditionalism bring destruction. So do arrogant ambitions and competition. We have to be willing to change when God points us in a new direction because the victory lies in that which God says. If you have the right attitude and are ready to change, you will find yourself where the power is and break through in everything you do.

6. The Principle of Protection

A strong defense is necessary both in physical and spiritual warfare. If you have ever played chess you know that you do not bring the queen out the first thing you do, even if that would mean that you easily would be able to knock out a pawn here and a pawn there. In chess, the queen is only brought out when she is protected. You do not strike using the queen until you know she is protected from every direction.

The same applies in both physical and spiritual warfare. You do not march out unless there is protection. Many have done so and returned defeated. But the worst thing a soldier can do is give up and return home. How can that be avoided? By marching out when the time is right and by doing it under protection.

To be protected in battle you have got to have information about your enemy. This is what we call intelligence.

..."lest Satan should take advantage of us; for we are *not ignorant of his devices*" (2 Cor 2:11)

If you are ignorant, Satan can take advantage of you. If you have knowledge of what your enemy is doing and what he is up to, you will have the advantage over him.

"Put on the full amour of God so that you can take your stand against the devil's schemes" (Eph 6:11 NIV).

The word for "schemes" that is used in the original Greek text means "methods". If you put on the armor, you can take your stand against the devil's methods—against his strategies, plans, goals and thoughts. The devil's methods are cunning and need to be exposed. How are they exposed? Through revelation knowledge.

In the prophet Elisha's day, the king of Syria was at war with Israel. When he and his servants planned an attack against Israel, he found time after time that the king of Israel already knew where the attack would take place, therefore was ready for it and could strike back. Finally, the king of Syria thought that Israel had a spy among his own men. But the officers answered him, *"None of us, my lord the king, but Elisha, the prophet who is in Israel, tells the king of Israel the very words you speak in your bedroom"* (2 King 6:12 NIV). The information that the prophet received, he gave directly to the king.

Jesus is king and prophet today. You have a part in His anointing. As a believer you have a tremendous advantage over your enemy. Through the Holy Spirit, God can give you all the information you need: "...He will tell you things to come" (Joh 16:13). Not only does He tell you what is going to happen, but also how you are to act in each situation.

7. The Principle of Surprise

The principle of surprise concerns three areas—time, method and place. *"But when the time had fully come, God sent his Son..."* (Gal 4:4 NIV). Jesus came to earth as a complete surprise to Satan, and this gave God the immediate advantage. The next surprise came on the day of Pentecost, when the Holy Spirit came upon the believers. That which happened at Pentecost was terrifying sight for the devil. The devil had seen *one* light walking about, and now the light was falling on thousands upon thousands of people.

Revival always comes as a surprise. When studying revival history you discover that nobody could predict whom God would use and to which denomination or place revival would come. Many times what happened would be what the people had least expected: *"Can anything good come out of Nazareth?"* (John 1:46) If we walk with God *we* become surprises. If we are not sensitive to God, we will fail to understand when God does something new. We have to constantly be ready for surprises.

There is tremendous power in a surprise attack, for the enemy does not have time to mobilize against it. Several hundred years passed before the devil could stop the supernatural in the first church. If we continue walking with God there will constantly be new surprises and the devil will be paralyzed.

8. The Principle of Cooperation

If we do not coordinate our activities, we will sooner or later start shooting at each other. For this reason it is important that we cooperate. We have different assignments but the same overall goal.

When we talk of fellowship and cooperation, we are not talking about everybody doing the exact same thing. Instead, it is a matter of us having been appointed by the Holy Spirit to do different things, that we agree on this, and that we do everything with a common purpose. If we cannot see the different tasks and their importance, we start looking askance at each other.

9. The Principle of Relief

As an army advances, it needs relief—food, ammunition, fuel and other necessities. The relief has to constantly follow the army. For this reason, there is something which in the military is called baggage. Every victory is temporary, if there is no relief which can make the victory permanent. When you attack, your enemy can back off in order to have time to regroup. By the time you have advanced and are weary, he has managed to arrange his troops and is ready to defeat you—while you stand there without fuel, ammunition and food. You won, but could not keep the victory.

Charles XII (King of Sweden 1697-1718), Napoleon Bonaparte and Adolf Hitler are responsible for three great fiascos in war history. These were known to be great generals and strategists, yet they failed.

Charles XII renewed the art of warfare of his time with considerably lighter combatant units. Napoleon was a strategist to his fingertips. He was a master of flexibility. No one could move an army and surprise as he could. Hitler was the inventor of the lightening attack, with demonic expertise in surprise attacks. But all three made the same mistake. They went into Russia with the purpose of "eating up the entire Russian bear". They continued marching in, bit by bit, and the Russians continued to back. At the same time, the Russians burned their wheat crops and all the food stores. It looked as though the Russians would lose. Finally, they reached the outskirts of Moscow. Winter came. And there they stood, teeth chattering, with an army of several hundred thousand men and without winter clothing or food. They had planned on eating the food the retreating Russians left behind, but the Russians saw to it that there was no food to be found. In addition, they had run out of fuel, the cold had set in and the soldiers started dying like flies. The Russians hardly needed to do a thing because these armies perished anyway by themselves. These were the most crushing defeats in war history.

Why did this happen? Well, they did not think about relief, that they needed coverage for their own needs. They became intoxicated with their successes and thought they had won the victory only because they were moving forwards.

You do not have the victory only because you are moving forwards. It may, however, *look* like a victory. The devil can, for instance, back and give in, maybe during a revival campaign, because he knows it will only last a few days or weeks. During this time, his troops find it too hot to endure, but as soon as the evangelist has left, they return.

For this reason, it is important to make sure the fruit is fruit that remains. The newly saved must get into the church and be fed the Word of God. It is not enough that they raised their hand to an invitation. You do not know if they really accepted Jesus or if they only raised their hand. You do not know if they merely confessed it with their mouth or if they confessed it with their mouth *and* believed it in their heart. You only know that after a few weeks. Then you see if they are still there.

One cannot assert that if children are simply given birth to, they will survive. They will only survive if they are given food and care. Thus it is extremely important that one does not let oneself by hypnotized by short-term results. Rejoice over them, but not too much. If you do, you will be disappointed.

The crucial question when having a campaign in a church is not what happens when you are there, but what happens when you have left. What happens to the newly saved? This is the big problem when it comes to revival campaigns, and there is an excellent solution to this problem. However, that solution will cost you sweat and work. You need to send in vanguards. If you are to hold a big campaign, you need to send people to that place months in advance, who search through the terrain, find faithful workers and train a team of follow-up workers, who are set on fire. When the evangelist then arrives, they will know exactly what to do in order for the fruit to be fruit that remains.

Revival campaigns can be useless, if you are unable to take care of the harvest. If people leave the church, the reason may not be that nobody took care of them.

10. The Principle of Retreat

There are times when you need to make a tactical retreat. This does not mean that you lose, compromise or give up. It means that you see a greater goal ahead and in order to reach this goal you have to redistribute your strength, recuperate and motivate your people once again. Maybe the battle has been so tough on one front that you save more, help more people and, in the long-run, win a greater victory, if you retreat in a certain area.

On the other hand, pride and arrogance can prevent people from retreating. This can ruin the whole work, instead of people regaining strength, going out again with greater power and breaking through on another front.

Johan Baner, one of the Swedish generals in the Thirty Years' War, was known for his ability to quickly beat a retreat and slip out of the enemy's treacherous traps. On one well-known occasion he quickly evacuated his entire army across a river. When the enemy came, he was long gone. His comment was, "The enemy thought he had me in the sack, but he had forgotten to tie the knot."

Similarly, the British retreat at Dunkerque during World War Two was actually a mass-rescue of thousands of soldiers, which later made possible the invasion of Normandy, and the allies' final victory over Hitler.

5

Take New Territory

In the Christian life, we go from glory to glory, but also from affliction to affliction. When you are a newborn baby in Christ, the Lord does not expect too much of you. Instead, He protects you from a lot. The first epistle of John 2:14 talks about children, young men and fathers. As you grow you receive a greater area of responsibility. When you receive that you also meet greater spiritual opposition. The smaller your area of responsibility, the smaller the attacks that come against you.

God often trains you in difficult circumstances. So in situations where you cannot see any results whatsoever, where you do not think anything is moving forward, where you do not believe your prayers are reaching all the way up to heaven, you can still be very strong in God. You might feel as though you have no contact with Him, but you do all the same.

If you do not give up, God will sometimes—only to encourage you—place you in a different situation. You may, for instance, find yourself among people who really long to hear about what you have received.

What happens then, is that which you have on the inside, that which you unconsciously have developed, flows out of you like a mighty river. You wonder where it is coming from, but it has been there all the time. When things were a bit difficult, arduous and trying, God, without you noticing it, developed your strength. To encourage you He places you in another situation where this comes forth.

From Glory to Glory

In the Old Testament the word "glory" is used about kings of distinction. The word is related to dignity, authority, power and responsibility. When the Word says that we go from glory to glory, this means that we go from a smaller field of responsibility to a greater one. You do not start out as a general, you start as vice corporal. Then you rise in the ranks, from glory to glory and from responsibility to responsibility.

God has different tasks for us, but He will always—regardless of what you are to become—take you from responsibility to responsibility. Every new "area of responsibility" in your life will involve more responsibility, more difficulties and greater attacks.

Life is divided into different periods. God knows when it is time for you to enter a new phase. When it is time for something new, the Holy Spirit starts preparing you for that change. He starts making you restless, so that you do not fall asleep in the nest. Young eagles have a wonderful time in the nest their mother prepared for them. In the end the mother has to force them to start flying by pushing them off the cliff edge. They will not fly voluntarily.

When things start getting too nice and comfortable it is easy to fall asleep. You enjoy the warmth and think everything is good as it is. When God wants to get you to understand that there is more glory, the Holy Spirit begins to pull at you. When the devil discovers what is about to happen, he is filled with fear. He is afraid of authority.

After all, the authority we have received is permission to destroy his kingdom.

The devil tries to interpret the signs of the times in your life and in that way calculate what is about to happen. If he cannot hinder the development, he tries to delay it. Every time it is time for you to be promoted in the spirit, you can count on the devil intensifying the attacks in your life. You may feel as if you are going backwards and as if you have failed completely, but in reality it is a sign of progress.

Constant Preparedness

Attack is the best defence. For this reason, the devil is anxious to attack you before you have broken through and reached the position where you can come against him with an even greater power. When you experience a breakthrough or a greater victory of some sort in your life, you must count on a great attack back at you. You will miss God and be severely beaten if you are not prepared for this.

What separated Gideon's three hundred men from those God sent home, was that they were watchful in the spirit and constantly were prepared to use their strength. They were watchful even when they ate and drank.

When you relax after a great victory, the devil is immediately there to recover territory or to torment you because God used you. The responsibility you will receive as a servant of the Lord will only increase—so will the victories. This means that the opposition against you also will be greater than ever.

Therefore, the Word say, *"Not many of you should presume to be teachers, my brothers…"* (Jam 3:1 NIV). You cannot step into a spiritual position if you are not ready for it. The most foolish thing one can do is try to force one's way into a ministry one is not ready for. This does not only concern young servants of the Lord, but also those who have been on the way for some time and whose ministries see signs and wonders.

If you start acting in the flesh or force your way into something you still are not ready for, you are wandering outside God's protection. "A man can receive nothing unless it has been given to him from heaven" (Joh 3:27).

Await the Right Time

This also applies to such a thing as starting a church. God wants new churches to be started. But when you have started a new church and after several years still have no more than seven members, there is something wrong somewhere. Do not call it a church when it in actual fact only is a prayer group. Wait with proclaiming a church until the group is so large that in cannot be managed in any other way.

It can very well be God's will that it is to become a church, but we often do not know the exact times. If we then dash off, we only attract a lot of persecution. I am not only referring to human persecution, but also to persecution in the spirit world. The devil licks his lips and says, "Ha, ha, ha! Those people do not know what they are doing!"

This concerns every area of your life. For this reason God has a special anointing for every phase of your life and a special strength which you must get hold of. Then you will have the power for that special task, in which you train yourself and become strong.

In my contacts with other ministers I have seen, that when they have problems, these are almost always caused by them entering into something they should not have concerned themselves with. God was the one who told them *to* do it, but He did not say *when* they were to do it and *how* they were to do it. If God has not said when and how, that means you are to wait. Take opportunities when they come along, but do not throw yourself into things your spirit does not feel peace about. Do not let pride press you.

Guard yourself against unnecessary attacks. If you do that, the anointing, power and joy in your life will be preserved and multiplied. You do not need to end up in periods of being depressed, burnt out and tired. These are things which can be prevented. Many of these problems are the result of poor discipline and lack of foresight. In war you cannot afford to only think of that which lies just beyond your nose. You must also think about that which lies behind the next bend. Be constantly watchful.

Every Victory has a Price

"Finally, be strong in the Lord and in his mighty power" (Eph 6:10 NIV). With greater responsibility come greater attacks. Therefore you also need more strength. If you want small attacks on your life, stay where you are. Do nothing more than what you are doing now. As soon as the Holy Spirit starts talking to you about taking steps into new areas, you can count on the counterattacks intensifying.

Every victory you win has a price. You may have fought hard to win. Then weariness can come against you and if you do not watch out you will become tired and be beaten time after time. Everybody can tolerate one defeat, but not constant defeat. Finally you just think, "This has to come to an end eventually!"

But the fact is, that if you do something for God, the opposition will never end. It will not end before you get to heaven. The devil will not quit tormenting you, before you are at home with God. Then he will no longer be able to reach you.

You have to be prepared to fight all your life. You can develop your strength in the Lord so that you enjoy the battle, because it will last as long as you are on earth.

Sometimes we say that we are going to take Europe and win it for Jesus. It is like digging a cave in Mount Everest with a teaspoon. We cannot do it in a day. Taking Europe cannot be done with three hearty shouts and a banner. There are enormous strongholds in the spiritual world which need to be demolished through persevering prayer, before Europe can be taken.

Do Not Make Any Comparisons!

We meet different types of opposition in different situations and places. You do not know the opposition, demons and principalities of other places. For this reason, you cannot take your own results and compare them with anybody else's. The strength is shown in different ways.

You might look at the great world evangelists and see all the people coming to their meetings, being saved, filled with the Spirit and healed. Then you end up in a village in some sparsely populated area. You start holding meetings but there is not at all the same swing as on the video cassettes you have been watching. The devil comes and tells you, "You are worthless. What kind of nonsense is this? There are no results. Compare yourself to him or her."

Never make comparisons like that, ever! It robs you of your strength. Do not compare yourself with anybody else, only with your own development from year to year and see in that way how you grow. The Word says, *"Each one should test his own actions. Then he can take pride in himself, without comparing himself to somebody else, for each one should carry his own load"* (Gal 6:4-5 NIV). When we are encouraged to *"be strong in the Lord and in his mighty power"*, that strength is for us to be able to carry our load, whichever yoke that has been placed upon our shoulders.

Sometimes the word "yoke" is used with reference to the devil, to describe the burden he has placed upon us (eg Is 9:4). Jesus releases us from this yoke. But we can also see how this word is used several times in the Old Testament in relation to God. Ecclesiastes talks about it, and so do the Psalms. A yoke is a tool with which one carries heavy burdens and which makes the carrying easier. God has a yoke for you. It is the task you are to do, the burden you are to carry. Everybody has their own burden. But Jesus says, *"For my yoke is easy and my burden is light"* (Matt 11:30 NIV).

Be strong in the Lord and in his mighty power. The power is for you to be able to carry your yoke; do not compare this to anybody else's yoke. If you are in a small place you can be stirred up and encouraged by what God is doing through other servants of the Lord, but be watchful of starting to compare yourself with them. God has not given you the task, the anointing and the burden to carry, that He has given them. He has given you something different, and you have received the strength to carry it. You will manage to carry it. Nobody else can carry it for you.

Maybe you are in a place where there are powerful religious strongholds and where a very small number of people are born-again Christians. If that is the case and you do what Jesus has asked you to do and break through so that a few people are saved, you may not realize how much that is worth. You cannot measure your results by comparing them to somebody else's. A breakthrough in the spirit with the power God has placed at your disposal, is worth a great deal, in whichever way this is manifested.

We praise God for all results, and we will have great results. We do not claim that only the invisible is important. But we are talking of what really happens in the spiritual world when you experience opposition from every direction and do not see the results you would like to see.

The key to victory is that you learn to use what is on the inside of you to break down opposition. You may not see such a great difference, but you will feel experience the freedom. The power in you breaks through the opposition around you.

6

The Believer's Armor

"Finally, my brethren, be strong in the Lord and in the power of His might. Put on the whole armor of God, that you may be able to stand against the wiles of the devil. For we do not wrestle against flesh and blood, but against principalities, against powers, against the rulers of the darkness of this age, against spiritual hosts of wickedness in the heavenly places. Therefore take up the whole armor of God, that you may be able to withstand in the evil day, and having done all, to stand. Stand therefore, having girded your waist with truth, having put on the breastplate of righteousness, and having shod your feet with the preparation of the gospel of peace; above all, taking the shield of faith with which you will be able to quench all the fiery darts of the wicked one. And take the helmet of salvation, and the sword of the Spirit, which is the word of God; praying always with all prayer and supplication in the Spirit, being watchful to this end with all perseverance and supplication for all the saints..." (Eph 6:10-18)

This is the armor God has given us. Verse 11 says that you are to take up the *whole* armor of God. Just as in the natural, it is something *you* have to do. You do not think about having to dress yourself, because it is a habit your have. You just do it and it is the exception if you do not do it yourself.

You need to put on *all* the parts of the armor. Just as you are to preach the full Gospel, you are to take on the whole armor. One of the devil's main means of weakening the body of Christ is to take away certain parts of the entirety, so that the Gospel is reduced.

Many committed Christians have been battled down. A zealous and committed Christian who is not wearing the armor, will be shot down in spite of his dedication. Dedication does not give you immunity. Anointing does not give you immunity either. You being committed does not mean that you will not be attacked. You being an anointed minister or in the ministry does not mean that you cannot be shot, wounded or even killed.

Great confusion can arise when believers see other devout Christians fail. Maybe you are thinking of your aunt who prayed to Jesus all her life and who really was a dedicated Christian. Suddenly she dies and nobody understands what really happened. You would have thought that if anyone would receive answers to prayer, it would have been your aunt, who prayed constantly and was so pious. I am sure she was a wonderful and godly lady, but that did not give her immunity. You can pray and be pious and still be very attacked. If anything, you will be even more attacked when you pray.

Many run off without the armor. Then, when they are shot they blame God, "If God had wanted to heal anybody it would have been my aunt. Because I am not at all as pious as my aunt, I cannot be healed, since she was not." This episode becomes a sort of monument, raised for the devil, which reminds these people that the power of God does not work. "If it did not work for my aunt, it will not work for anybody."

What you did not see in the spirit world was that maybe she was not wearing the armor. She may not have been living in sin, but the only knowledge she had was of the helmet of salvation. If you have knowledge of the whole armor you live differently.

The Helmet of Salvation

Every part of the armor has a name and refers to a certain part of the atonement or Christian life. The first part is the helmet of salvation. Many Christians do not know if they are born-again. In certain churches, saying that you *know* you are a child of God, is seen as arrogance.

But the assurance of which family you belong to shields you from confusion. If you, in the natural, do not know which family you belong to, you will be confused. Assurance produces security. The helmet of salvation gives you security and protection. It creates assurance and security in your life and mind which keeps you from confusion. It protects your thoughts from attacks.

Salvation is absolutely the most important thing for a human being. But salvation entails so much more than being born again. Being born again is the beginning of salvation. If the only thing you are sure of is your salvation, you are, in the eyes of God, like a soldier standing on the battlefield, naked but with a helmet on his head.

When one thinks about it in this way, it is easier to understand why so many Christians live in defeat. It has nothing to do with dedication. You can be committed to Jesus and be willing to serve Him, but if you do not do as He says, you will be like a naked soldier. You will be a target for the devil, easily shot down.

Above all, the helmet of salvation protects your thoughts. Ninety-five percent of all your problems owe to you thinking in the wrong way. You have more problems with your thoughts than anything else. That is where the great problems lie.

"For those who sleep, sleep at night, and those who get drunk, get drunk at night. But since we belong to the day, let us be self-controlled, putting on faith and love as a breastplate, and the hope of salvation as a helmet" (1 Tess 5:7-8 NIV).

Just as faith has to do with the shield, the helmet is connected with hope. Hope and faith are not the same thing. Faith receives now. Hope expects something in the future. Hope is a joyful expectation and assurance that something is going to happen. Hope is the last thing to leave a human being. People do not die before they have given up hope of living. Hope is a motivational force in your life, just as faith is. Hope is necessary, but should not be confused with faith.

We have an anchor of hope thrown onto the other side of the veil, just as a boat in a storm that is entering the harbor. In order to get out of a storm, you have to throw out an anchor and pull yourself towards the harbor and peace and quiet. Hope is an expectation that something is going to change—an anticipation of the future. You need to be constantly expectant.

See to it that people do not lose hope, become indifferent or get stuck in a rut. People do become desperate in certain situations, but there is also another type of hopelessness. Hope is then not working as a spiritual power, and people become satisfied and indifferent.

Contentment is to praise God no matter what things look like around you. It is assurance that what you see now is not final. You need contentment so that you do not become frustrated. You can also be content in another way, and this is more closely related to indifference, a type of apathy. This is a spiritual disease, which comes against every church.

In hope, there is a power which pulls down the anointing. In hope there is a glad expectation of what God is going to do, which is aimed at the future. It constantly pulls you forward and protects your thought-life when you are attacked. It is a solid power which guards your mind when the devil is lying to you.

At the time of the shipwreck which takes place in Acts 27:21-22, Paul says,

"Men, you should have listened to me, and not have sailed from Crete and incurred this disaster and loss. And now I urge you to take heart, for there will be no loss of life among you, but only of the ship" (Acts 27:21-22)

Paul encouraged the crew to take heart and to start hoping again. Hope is the starter and faith is the actual motor. You have to get the hope going in order to be able to activate the faith. You need to get people to take heart before you pray for them with results. Them taking heart does not mean that they are blissfully happy and jump up and down, but that the hope is starting to be ignited in them. Faith cannot start working before hope has been ignited in a person. When the hope in your life is turned into hopelessness it is difficult to do anything.

People who are sick need hope in their lives. Do not take their hope away from them. If you meet people with serious diseases, you need to find out what they are feeling. Some feel hopelessness, some have a spark of hope but no faith and some have faith. You have to minister to people on their level.

It is better to teach people for an hour from the Word of God and then to pray for five minutes, than to teach for five minutes and pray for an hour. You can pray for five hours and not have the person with you. But if the person is in agreement with you, the results start to come. Hope gets the healing process started. We need to give hope to the people who do not get healed at campaigns, and work on a longer-term basis, because God does want to see them healed. Your task is to get them to take heart.

You need the helmet of salvation as protection for your mind when the devil says that it will not work. For as long as you live, your mind will be bombarded with the thought that nothing is going to succeed. Use the law of contrast—when the devil says that something is impossible to carry out, it is proof that God says it is possible. The more the devil screams that you are going to fail, the greater is the chance that you will succeed. What the devil says is always a lie. For this reason you cannot listen to him day in, day out. You have to protect your thought-life every day.

The Breastplate of Righteousness

When Paul speaks of the armor, he is thinking of the Roman soldier's suit of armor. The Romans had a protection for the chest, but no protection for the back. The Roman soldiers were taught never to turn their backs on anything. As an external constraint for them never to go backwards but always forwards, they had no protection for the back. The breastplate covers the most important parts of your body. It covers the bowels, the heart, lungs and stomach. It covers the entire inner life. The consciousness and confession that you are righteous through Jesus Christ protects all of your inner life.

"...as sin reigned in death, even so grace might reign through righteousness to eternal life through Jesus Christ our Lord" (Rom 5:21).

Either you are strong in the Lord and in His power, or some other power will be strong against you. Through death, sin exerts a pressure against people. But in this life grace through righteousness will wield its kingdom and its dominance against Satan.

Righteousness is a power and a protection for you but a threat to the devil. You exert pressure on the devil's kingdom by walking in righteousness. When you know that you have been made righteous and are not constantly tormented by condemnation, righteousness will give you security.

The breastplate offers good protection. It gives your inner being room to grow strong. Freedom from condemnation is the most important thing you have. The devil is called the accuser. He accuses you as much as he can every day until you tell him to stop. If you sin the blood of Jesus will cleanse you. You must clothe yourself in righteousness every day. You have to confess that you are made righteous and actively stir it up.

Why do so many pastors quit their ministry? Why do so many Christians give up? Because they never put on the breastplate of righteousness. There was nothing to stop the devil from contaminating their spirit. There was nothing to stop the devil from hindering the outflow from their spirits. He got at them from the inside, because they were under constant condemnation.

Condemnation has been preached from the pulpits of Sweden for many years. Many believers in our nation have lived with condemnation and the devil has thus stripped entire churches. He has stolen thousands of breastplates. And people wonder why God allows one affliction after another! The answer is that we have been exposed and robbed of our weapons, and that is an abomination.

An army without breastplates, which is full of condemnation and apologizes for everything, can never do anything for God. This is why not much has happened in the Christian Church. In order to protect your inner life and to be able to advance powerfully, you need to wear the breastplate and be established in righteousness. This does not mean being superior or cocky, but having a sound boldness because God has given you, as a gift, the righteousness of Jesus, which you are free to use, because God truly *wants* this. Because of Jesus, God has by grace given you a right relationship to Himself, without a feeling of inferiority, guilt or shame.

The Shoes of the Readiness of the Gospel of Peace

"...having shod your feet with the preparation of the gospel of peace..." (Eph 6:15)

Shoes are meant for walking in. God is eager for you to go. For you to be able to go, you need a goal. You have that goal through your hope and thoughts. If you do not have a goal, you will either walk in circles or sit still. Both alternatives are just as wrong. You are always to be on your way somewhere, and with the purpose of spreading the gospel.

Through your feet you have contact with this earth. This means that the primary contact you have with this world and its system is there for you to spread the gospel to them. You are living in the kingdom of God and the contacts you have with non-Christians are for you to be able to bring them into the kingdom of God. The methods may vary, but the purpose is clear.

Jesus was the friend of both publicans and sinners, but he spent time with them with the purpose of getting them into the kingdom of God. If you are to be more effective you too must mix with people who do not believe in Jesus. When you no longer have any non-Christian contacts, nor are eager to have them, you have chucked your shoes off. Without shoes, you get wounded, dirty feet.

The Shield of Faith

The shield is a powerful weapon of defence. Paul says that faith has the ability to extinguish all the flaming arrows of Satan. Temptations and compromises invite the world to enter in and the result is weakness and defeat. But faith, the measure of faith which God has given all Christians (Rom 12:3), resists the devil. Unbelief and doubt deteriorate and flee.

The first epistle of John 5:4-5 says that faith overcomes the world. This means that faith blocks everything the devil, the world and the flesh hurl against a believer in order to tempt, weaken, break and dishearten him. Faith can stop *all* the flaming arrows of the evil one, thus the enemy hates faith. Faith sees Jesus, His work on the cross, His righteousness, His gifts and His love, when everything seems dark and hopeless.

Faith is not an invention of the flesh, but a gift from God. Faith is the God-given inherent power which casts mountains into the sea, sees the answer to prayer long before it comes, receives forgiveness, deliverance, healing and victory from God, when circumstances and feelings point in a completely different direction. Through faith we overcome our enemies. Hebrews 11:34 says, *"...out of weakness were made strong, became valiant in battle, turned to flight the armies of the aliens"*.

The Gospel of Mark 9:23 says, "Everything is possible for him who believes" (NIV). In the most bitter and difficult of battles faith has the ability to turn defeat into victory and the attacks of Satan into flight, at the same time as his flaming arrows are quenched. Without the shield of faith we do not stand a chance in the battle. Therefore there is a tremendous need for faith teaching, so that the believer—by walking in faith—can live in victory.

The Sword of the Spirit

The sword of the Spirit is really the only pure weapon of attack. The sword of the Spirit is the living Word of God. It is God's promises to you and me. God's promises are very precious. 2 Peter 1:4 says,

"Through these he has given us his very great and precious promises, so that through them you may participate in the divine nature and escape the corruption in the world caused by evil desires" (NIV).

In other words, the promises give us both a part of God's nature and victory over the attacks of the enemy.

Faith comes through the promises, the Word (Rom 1:17). God performs miracles through the promises, and through you holding on to them. Abraham believed in God's promises and God gave, contrary to the circumstances, him and Sarah a son, Isaac. Hebrews 6:12 says that we through faith and patience inherit the promises. How will it happen? Through us holding on to the Word, the promises!

The Word is a sword which exposes the motives of our hearts and sorts out the thoughts which are not from God (Hebr 4:12). The Word is a sword that drives away Satan's temptations, just as when Jesus answered Satan with the written Word in the Gospel of Matthew 4:10, *"Away from me, Satan! For it is written..."* (NIV)

Nothing in the universe is more powerful than the word of God. When you believe, receive, understand, confess and use the word of God, Satan has not got a chance against you. He is driven away and you advance. He retreats and you see the promises become reality in your life through God's covenant-faithfulness to His own word.

The Belt of Truth

In Paul's day people wore a long wide garment closest to the body. The different parts of the armor were put on over the garment and finally everything was fastened together with the help of a wide belt, a girdle. Everything was supported by this belt which held together all the other parts of the armor.

If you have all the other parts of the armor but do not have the belt of truth, everything hangs loose. Nothing works. The belt gives it all stability, temperance and discipline. Everything is held together by the belt. This is the task of truth.

When you leave truth, you are skating on thin ice. The Word says that the truth sets us free (Joh 8:32). The aim of truth is for you to be set free. If you are walking in untruth in any area of your life, you are not free in that area. The truth will set you free—the truth about who God is, who your enemy is and who you are.

If you have an incorrect picture of who God is, you will get wrong results. If you have an incorrect picture of yourself, the results will also be wrong. There are two ditches here. One is that you underestimate yourself. The other is that you overestimate yourself.

You need to have a realistic picture of yourself. If you do not, you will end up in half-truth and lies and this will harm your spiritual life.

When the truth about something reaches you, you have to be willing to receive it, no matter which direction or through whom it arrives. People often choose which truths they want to receive and through which channels the truth is to come. I once heard a person in a position of leadership say, "There is no reason to listen to Kenneth Hagin; if God wants to tell us something, He will do it through prophets of our own ranks".

There is only one "rank" and that is the rank in the body of Christ. The Word says furthermore, *"The wind (the Spirit) blows wherever it pleases... So it is with everyone born of the Spirit"* (Joh 3:8 NIV). You have no right to limit God with your own ideas about things. If you set up prerequisites for accepting the truth, you are already bound by lies.

God—not you—decides who He wants to use and how and when He wants to do so.

If Bileam had to listen to a donkey (Num 22), you too might have to listen to a "donkey". Bileam did not expect to receive revelation in that way, but when he would not listen, this finally became the only way in which God could speak to him.

You do not know from which direction God is going to speak to you, but you can know when God is the one speaking to you, because of the inner testimony. Make a decision to accept what God says *when* He speaks. You have to be able to receive it, whether it comes from somebody who is more or less spiritual than you and irrespective of it that person is superior or subordinate to you.

The truth also has to do with temperance. This means that you watch yourself. *"Watch your life and doctrine closely. Persevere in them, because if you do, you will save both yourself and your hearers"* (1 Tim 4:16 NIV). Be conscientious with your life. Do not be careless. Watch out for "pious gossip". See to it that you do not tell half-truths and that you do not cast suspicion on people or slander them, because if you start living in such a way, the entire armor will start flapping and people around you will notice that.

The belt of truth has a restraining, stabilizing effect upon your life. When you walk in truth, you walk in self-discipline; you watch what you say, how you say it and when you say it. You are careful with speaking the truth yourself and only listen to that which is true. It is necessary for a soldier to possess self-discipline. He cannot have a bunch of views, thoughts and ideas which he constantly chatters about. He has to be restrained in his speech. Be slow to speak and quick to listen (Jam 1:19).

You may have erroneous ideas and a lacking knowledge, but if you are careful in this area, God will always bless you. The belt is meant to hold everything together and to protect you, so that there are no gaps. If you are mindful of truth, God will always honor you, bless you and multiply your ministry.

Prayer and Supplication

The entire armor is to be put on during prayer, supplication, praise and intercession. Prayer is the oil of the machinery, the gasoline in the tank, the wind in the sails. The life of prayer is a whole world, into which we can enter—wonderful, fascinating and exciting. In an upcoming chapter I will discuss some aspects of the world of prayer. Without prayer you have no life with God. In the same way that one cannot live without breathing, it is impossible to be a victorious believer without praying.

When the armor is in place you are equipped with something tremendously effective and powerful. Do not forget what Paul says about it:

"For the weapons of our warfare are not carnal but mighty in God for pulling down strongholds, casting down arguments and every high thing that exalts itself against the knowledge of God, bringing every thought into captivity to the obedience of Christ" (2 Cor 10:4-5).

7

The Significance of a Strong Defence

Even though we are called to go forward and conquer new territories, the truth is that the emphasis is really on defense. This means that the key to victory in your life is a strong defence.

We are offensive, but we are so on the basis of a strong defensive position. We do not go out and fight without being sure of our position. I once read in a book that defence is better than attack. I reacted against this and thought that it surely cannot be biblical. But then I turned to Ephesians 6 and to my surprise discovered that the main emphasis in that chapter is on defence.

Verse 10: *"Be strong in the Lord and in his mighty power"* (NIV)—both offensive and defensive

Verse 11: *"Stand against the devil's schemes"* (NIV)—defensive

Verse 12: *"Our struggle"* (NIV)—offensive and defensive

Verse 13: *"Therefore take up the whole armor of God, that you may be able to withstand"*—defensive: somebody attacks and you withstand.

Verse 13: *"stand your ground"* (NIV)—defensive: you protect what you have conquered.

The armor consists chiefly of weapons of defence:

The shield of faith—defense
The helmet of salvation—defense
The breastplate of righteousness—defense
The belt of truth—defense
Shoes of the readiness of the gospel of peace—offensive
The sword of the Spirit—offensive

"Finally, be strong in the Lord and in his mighty power. Put on the full amour of God so that you can take your stand against the devil's schemes" (Eph 6:10-11 NIV)

When we talk of spiritual warfare, we are talking of attack. We attack the kingdom of Satan. We attack him consistently, on all occasions and in every place. We are continually on the offensive. We constantly take new initiatives and push aside the kingdom of darkness. This is the basic attitude of the church. We are not fighting a war of survival, we are attacking. This attitude is imparted to you through the Holy Spirit.

It is said that attack is the best defence. There is a lot of truth in that, for when we attack, the opponent has to defend himself. The danger Christians face is that we *only* defend ourselves, in other words that we constantly lie five to ten years behind everybody else. Therefore, our fundamental attitude should be that we take the initiative.

Surprises are very discomfiting to the devil. He cannot calculate what God plans to do. For this reason, God's actions often come as a surprise to him. They are like a bombshells because he is not ready for them. When there has been an attack against his kingdom, he has to reorganize and counterattack, which he naturally attempts to do. At this point he uses special weapons, for example getting people stuck in a rut and indifference, to put a stop to the attack from heaven.

We are offensive. That is our basic attitude. The fact remains, however, that the battle we are fighting often is about a war of defense. In all types of war, the war has always been won thanks to a strong defense. Having a strong defense does not mean that you are solely defensive and never attack. It simply means that you constantly defend what you have conquered, while moving onwards.

Do not Forget the Defense!

In the early stages of a preacher's ministry, the invitations are usually pretty few and far in between. There can be a long period of time before you get an invitation to preach, and you wonder why nobody summons you. But then you suddenly receive a call. You pray a lot about this and finally it is time to go. Things are wonderful because you have prepared the whole thing in prayer for months. People are blessed and very happy. Not only can you return to that place, but the report spreads, so that others call you too. The telephone starts going warm and all of a sudden you are booked for a long time to come.

What then happens is that you become so booked and so occupied with doing battle and being offensive, that the devil is just waiting for an opportunity to finish you off. At this point you are busy "shooting" every day, in several directions, but after a while the ammunition starts running out. If you do not watch it, you will be worn out. Your spiritual strength will slowly start to leave you.

All these invitations will then become opportunities for the devil to tire you out and strike you down when you attack. He lets you into enemy territory and entices you to attack. Everything seems to be clear, so you continue, but you do not know that the enemy has backed with all his troops and now waits a few miles ahead. When you have charged ahead with top speed, and your gasoline, ammunition and food have run out on his territory, he comes tearing with everything he has. He attacks you with depression, family strife, disputes with other ministries and by putting your anointing and even your ministry in question.

This is the battery that comes against you when you have been out in the weekends, swinging yourself in the liana of the Spirit. When you come home, you let go of the liana and crash-land. You do not want to talk to anybody for several days and are grumpy and angry.

This torments many preachers during their entire lives, especially if they are traveling preachers. This is tragic, and not how God wants it to be.

Things like this happen when you advance without having a strong defense. You have not yet realized that most wars have been won thanks to a strong defense, not only through glamorous campaigns. If you understand this, you will direct your energy toward always having a strong defense in your own personal life.

Be Prepared for Counterattack!

When you win a victory you want to rest in the aftermath of that victory. You want to enjoy the sweets of victory. But that is highly dangerous.

When a meeting has been concluded, irrespective of size or dimension, it is over. That which has been done and won is past and has to be left for that which is ahead. You can remember what happened, so that you can testify about it, but leave it behind you and start praying for the next meeting.

Build yourself up and prepare yourself, for each victory and attack is always succeeded by a counter-attack. In Acts 16 we read about how Paul cast a spirit of divination out of a girl. He wins a victory, but immediately there is a counter-attack. It came through those who had earned money through the girl with the spirit of divination. It was no small attack. The entire city was in uproar, and Paul and Silas were dragged to the judges, who threw them in jail. This was the counter-attack Paul experienced for casting out an evil spirit.

The purpose of showing you this is not to fill you with fear. We are not to fearfully expect a terrible blow after each victory. But we must be aware of these counter-attacks, because it is when we relax after a victory that the devil comes to flatten us. If we, at that point, have a strong defense, he will not even be able to get within the walls.

This is how wars are won. At the same time as you are offensive, you make sure to build up a strong defense. This is important for you personally, for your prayer group, for your church and for your mission organization and so on.

If you do not have a strong defense, you will—no matter how many and how great your victories have been—become a "yo-yo-Christian". The devil will pester and torment you in proportion to your victories. In the end everything will feel difficult and somewhere along the way you will say, "This is not worth the price. Every time I do something of any value for God, things get miserable".

This is an indication of it being time to back up and build up the defense. When all the invitations come—or whatever it is you are involved in—you need to check what God has asked you to do and get a clear picture of what you need to commit yourself to.

Learn To Sort Out what is not of God

You will always have more to do than you can handle—for then you have to trust God and cannot take the glory yourself. It is a lifestyle which you just have to get used to. You can be relaxed in the midst of all the work. You can learn to rest—physically, mentally and spiritually—while you are working.

Do not make work your enemy. Do not whine about everything you have to do. God will require of you that you do much. The devil will also send a lot in your way. For this reason, you have to learn to sort out what is of God and what is not. But you will always have plenty to do.

Satan will try to weigh you down and tire you out, but you cannot win the victory by fleeing every exertion. You must learn to tackle and get through it. You will not get through it by complaining about the circumstances. You do it by protecting yourself and having a strong defense. God will expect of you that you do far more than your natural capacity is sufficient for.

You will be given tasks which you will not have a clue as to how to solve. Then you have to trust the Holy Spirit, draw from Him and ask Him. You cannot always ask people. God is your strength, people are not.

God will teach you and take you through the difficulties. But you must learn to protect yourself, so that you can hear the Holy Spirit speaking. When you are tired, it is difficult to hear from God; when you are physically, mentally and spiritually run-down it is difficult to hear from God. At this point, all the circumstances have started choking the Word in your life and so it cannot bear fruit in the way God wants it to.

When this happens you have to start sorting. You may think that there is nothing you can cut down on, of what you are doing. But the key is not either that you stop doing a lot of things which you are doing; the key is that you stop worrying about these things.

When something becomes so important that you do not have time to spend with God, you must cut it off. It is more important to spend time with the Lord than to do anything for Him. There are things you will have to stop doing, but when you do so, you will discover that you still will get more to do all the time.

Do not try to comfort yourself or those around you by saying that things will be calmer next year. Do not let yourself be fooled by that lie. If you are being used by God, you will constantly have more to do.

But in all this you have to have a strong defense—when it comes to what you think about and especially where your time is concerned. Your time is the most important thing of all, for it will never come back. Failures concerning money and other such things can be remedied—but time, you will never get back.

8

Victory—Your Starting Position

You have been given a position of victory. You have received a crown of authority and the Word says, *"Hold on to what you have, so that no one will take your crown"* (Rev 3:11 NIV). You have been given life and blessings. Make sure the thief does not steal these from you.

The thief will not come to you, if you have nothing. He attacks you with sly schemes on the basis of you having something and being somebody. He wants to pull you down from the position of authority God has given you. The devil hates authority. He is an instigator of rebellion and hates the fact that you have a position above him. The prayer Paul prays in the first chapter of Ephesians talks very clearly about this (Eph 1:17-23).

This prayer is about you realizing what you have in Christ Jesus. You need to become conscious of the resources that are placed at your disposal. When you know of these, you do not need to be afraid, even if things around you start to shake.

You have to know how much is placed at your disposal. The devil wants to make you believe that nothing is placed at your disposal, that everything is deposited in heaven, available to you only when you get there. But you do not need any weapons in heaven. It is here you can make use of them.

Guard Your Position in Christ!

This revelation often seems to be the one most difficult for Christians to grasp. But the fact remains that God's power, in all its potential, is working daily upon and in you as a believer.

In Ephesians 1:21-23 we see that Christ is seated *"far above all principality and power and might and dominion, and every name that is named, not only in this age but also in that which is to come. And He put all things under His feet and gave Him to be the head over all things to the church, which is His body, the fullness of Him who fills all in all"*.

One does not separate the head from the body. Together they form a whole—a person. Every limb in the body of Christ is thus seated above the powers of darkness, just as Jesus Christ himself—the head—is.

God has given Jesus to the church. Jesus is the head. When Jesus is the head of His body, He fills the entire body, as we just read. This means that if everything is put under Jesus' feet, everything is put under our feet. He has no other feet than our feet, for we are His body. We are knitted together with Him through the Holy Spirit. We are the body of Christ on earth.

That is not to say that each one of us is Jesus Christ on earth. There is a tremendous difference between God and His creation. We are dust and we will die, but through the Holy Spirit God has imparted His nature to us. We are not equal to God, but we are in the same class as God, of the same type. God begets spirits. He is the Father of spirits (Hebr 12:9), so we are of the same kind as God. Because he has borne us again, we are His children.

The devil is very agitated about this. He wants to make God something obscure and distant, but God has come near us through Jesus Christ. By His grace He has, through the covenant, raised us up to His own level and seated us with Him in the heavenly places (Eph 2:6).

This does not give us any right to flaunt ourselves at God's expense. He is our Lord and our God. We worship Him. But we do not thereby deny our new identity in Christ Jesus. We thank God for the position He has given us, and we use it to spread the kingdom of God on earth.

It Is Easy to Defend Oneself When in the Superior Position

When you know your position, you have, regardless of what the circumstances look like at the time, an advantageous starting point. When people in former times were attacked by enemies, they climbed up onto a rock and were impossible to reach. The enemy could try to attack them in every way, but nobody dared to climb up. The fact is that if you are on top, it is easy to push down the person who tries to come up. But if you are down, it is very difficult to pull down the one who is on top.

The same principle applies to the business world. It is next to impossible to cut out a leading company. If you have a superior position and then defend this, it is very difficult for others to defeat you.

If you, for instance, have won a victory over spirits of poverty, hold on to that victory and do not become slack and indifferent, but cultivate and defend it, it will be very difficult for the devil to steal that victory from you.

Similarly, there are preachers who are very successful in certain areas. They can have an erroneous theology or be negligent in certain other things, but the victory nevertheless follows them throughout their entire lives. They have come into the spirit in those areas and got a superior position.

The same thing applies to you. When you have realized the position you have and start making use of that position, you will have an advantage in the area concerned. This advantage will last throughout your life—if you make sure you stand your ground. It is extremely difficult for the devil to take it away from you.

The Significance of War Songs

Several of the Psalms have their origins in war. Indeed, it is often in war that songs are birthed. Song and music are clearly associated with war and battle.

Songs of victory and battle have been sung in all times and cultures. It is something God has imparted to humanity. In certain cases it has been perverted by the devil, but the idea has its origin in God.

Through song you can stir up the gifts of grace which are in you. In the American Civil War, both the Northern and Southern states had their songs, and at least two of them are very well-known today. The Southerners' song was called "When Johnny Comes Marching Home". They sang that when Johnny—the soldiers—came home, everything would be alright once again. But when the Northern soldiers went out to war, they sang, "Glory, Glory Hallelujah, His Truth is Marching On". They actually sang of the glory of God.

This might have been a contributing reason to why the North won. One side sang of victory and the other sang about how nice it would be to come home.

Our churches do the exact same thing when they completely engage themselves in singing songs which only deal with how wonderful it is going to be to get home to heaven. The words can well be true, but the effect is devastating. *Only* singing songs of one's homeland is spiritual nostalgia—or spiritual escapism.

In every revival, songs have been sung. The Reformation was not won solely through Luther's preaching. It was sung into peoples' hearts. In the beginning, they had no idea of what they were singing about, when they sang, "A Mighty Fortress is Our God". But when they had sung the hymn a couple hundred times, their perception of God began to change. In that hymn Luther writes of Satan, "The prince of darkness grim, We tremble not for him; His rage we can endure, For lo! his doom is sure, one little word shall fell him".

When this is sung time and again something happens in our inner being. It becomes a battle song. The whole Bible is full of victory songs after battle—Miriam's song of victory (Ex 15:21), Deborah's song of victory (Judg 5), David's songs of victory (e.g. 2 Sam 22; Ps 9, 18, 21, 68) and many others.

Songs are vital for stirring up the people for battle, for winning the victory and then keeping the victory. This is why David wrote many psalms about war, battle and victory. Psalm 18 is an example of this:

"I will love You, O Lord, my strength. The Lord is my rock and my fortress and my deliverer; My God, my strength, in whom I will trust; My shield and the horn of my salvation, my stronghold. I will call upon the Lord, who is worthy to be praised; So shall I be saved from my enemies." Psalm 18:1-3

If you want to be saved from your enemies, do as David did. Remind yourself of who God is. Who is God? He is your strength. In this battle, God is your strength. Who is God? He is your rock. When you really are in need of protection, he is your protection. Who is God? He is your fortress. No enemy can enter that fortress. Who is God? He is your deliverer. He is your shield. He is the horn of your salvation.

In the Bible, the horn is a symbol of strength. The horn was used to pour out anointing. The horn was used as a cup and there was oil in it. One would take the horn from a bull, hollow it out, pour oil into it and anoint kings. This is a symbol of the strength in the Holy Spirit. When Samuel felt that everything was over, and he was tired and wanted to give up, God told him, *"Fill your horn with oil and be on your way; I am sending you to Jesse of Bethlehem. I have chosen one of his sons to be king"* (1 Sam 16:1 NIV). The oil is an symbol for new, fresh strength in your life.

Remind Yourself of Who God Is!

When you fight, you must remind yourself of what God is like. Read this from Psalm 18 and meditate upon what it means to you in the battle you are fighting:

"For by You I can run against a troop, by my God I can leap over a wall. As for God, His way is perfect; the word of the Lord is proven; He is a shield to all who trust in Him.

For who is God, except the Lord? And who is a rock, except our God? It is God who arms me with strength, and makes my way perfect. He makes my feet like the feet of deer, and sets me on my high places. He teaches my hands to make war, so that my arms can bend a bow of bronze.

You have also given me the shield of Your salvation; Your right hand has held me up, Your gentleness has made me great. You enlarged my path under me, so my feet did not slip. I have pursued my enemies and overtaken them; neither did I turn back against till they were destroyed. I have wounded them, so that they could not rise; they have fallen under my feet." (Ps 18:29-38)

This is a psalm. These are the hymns we should sing in church. When I was training to become a priest, I came in contact with several truly High Church people. One thing they strongly emphasized was the singing of Psalms. They would say, "Psalms is the hymn-book of the Church". They had grasped a truth and I learned this from them.

We have received an entire book of songs in the Bible. The hymns in Psalms are meant to be sung. These are better than many of the hymns of unbelief which can be found in the various songbooks of our time. Some of them seem to be demonically inspired—they are so full of unbelief and defeat. When you sing them, you make room for religious demons.

"For You have armed me with strength for the battle; You have subdued under me those who rose up against me. You have also given me the necks of my enemies, so that I destroyed those who hated me. They cried out, but there was none to save; even to the Lord, but He did not answer them. Then I beat them as fine as the dust before the wind; I cast them out like dirt in the streets.

You have delivered me from the strivings of the people; You have made me the head of the nations; a people I have not known shall serve me. As soon as they hear of me they obey me; the foreigners submit to me. The foreigners fade away, and come frightened from their hideouts.

The Lord lives! Blessed be my Rock! Let the God of my salvation be exalted. It is God who avenges me, and subdues the peoples under me; He delivers me from my enemies. You also lift me up above those who rise against me; you have delivered me from the violent man. Therefore I will give thanks to You, O Lord, among the Gentiles, and sing praises to Your name. Great deliverance He gives to His king, and shows mercy to His anointed, to David and his descendants forevermore." Ps 18:39-50

If David had lived today he would have been excommunicated for talking in this way. But this is the Bible, the Word of God. This is a warrior talking and we are to sing in the same way. This is what God will do in and through you, if you start making it your confession.

People are not our enemies. *"For we do not wrestle against flesh and blood, but against principalities, against powers, against the rulers of the darkness of this age, against spiritual hosts of wickedness in the heavenly places"* (Eph 6:12). In that battle, God has victory ready for you. Just like David, you need to remind yourself of who God is and what He has done for you. He is your strength, He is your fortress, He is your rock and He is your victory.

When you praise and worship Him, joy—the joy of victory—flows forth in your life and gives you strength in the battle. That joy can come in the most difficult of circumstances and sometimes completely surpass comprehension. But it gives an assurance of the love and presence of Jesus and faith for breakthrough and victory.

9

The Prayer of Travail

"Now it came about in the course of those many days that the king of Egypt died. And the sons of Israel *sighed* because of the bondage, and they *cried out*; and their *cry* for help because of their bondage rose up to God. So God heard their *groaning*; and God remembered His covenant with Abraham, Isaac and Jacob. God saw the sons of Israel, and God took notice of them" (Ex 2:23-25 NASB).

There are a few words here, in particular, that we are going to look more closely at. The words are *sighed*, *cried out* and *groaned*. In this chapter we will discuss a type of prayer which generally is called travailing prayer. We will explain why we pray in this way and the effect it has in the spirit world. Many people have questions concerning travailing prayer and wonder if one *must* pray in such a way. I believe the Holy Spirit wants to answer all these questions.

The Word of God talks of many different types of prayer. Prayer is like a tool box. You take out the tool you need for the moment. The Holy Spirit does the exact same thing. He takes out the prayer which is needed to achieve the best result in a certain situation. By doing that, the Holy Spirit helps you to pray.

When you and I were born again and came into the kingdom of God, we were born into a kingdom which is different from this world. Jesus says that the kingdom of

God is inside the person that is born again. God's Spirit lives in your spirit; your spirit is the new Man, your inner being. God wants to teach you that things do not always work the same way in the spiritual world as they do in the physical world, which we are accustomed to drawing our conclusions from.

When a human being starts living in society, he or she is formed and fostered by it. People around you do different things because of tradition and culture, things you as a believer are not always supposed to do. There are also certain types of unspoken laws—in a bus, for instance, many sit in silence, reading the evening newspaper, and one does not raise one's voice.

Your surroundings form you in a certain way. In reality, it is the spirit of this world putting a lid on people, to hinder them from coming out into freedom. Every human is created to live in freedom; our inner man is created for freedom.

Sighing, Crying and Groaning

In this chapter's introductory Bible verse, we saw that the children of Israel were not in freedom, but in captivity. But then they started to pray a certain type of prayer, the prayer of travail. The expression "travailing prayer" cannot be found in this Bible verse, but the meaning is there. Let me explain it to you.

If you go through the Word, you see that much is written about this type of prayer. However, you do not always think of that fact that what you are reading really is about prayer. When one hears the words "sighing", "crying" and "groaning", one does not think of prayer in the first place; one would be more inclined to think of somebody who goes around and complaining and thinking everything is wretched. That is not the kind of sighing the Bible is talking about. What the Bible is referring to here, is a type of prayer.

Travailing prayer actually includes a lot of different things. I aim to discuss different aspects of this subject, so that your mind will become more accustomed to this. You may have seen people pray in a way you have never seen before, and your mind is starting to set the brakes in motion. You think, "I could never behave like that. If I am to pray, it is to be quietly and calmly. I close my eyes, lift my hands. That is prayer to me."

But you have to know that prayer can mean many different things, depending on what is happening in the spirit world. The type of prayer the children of Israel prayed in Exodus 2:23 produced their deliverance. Their sighing, crying out and groaning rose up to God and he heard their cries. He thought of His covenant and delivered them. Travailing prayer produces deliverance.

In Judges, there is a similar verse:

"And when the Lord raised up judges for them, the Lord was with the judge and delivered them out of the hands of their enemies all the days of the judge; for the Lord was moved to pity by their groaning because of those who oppressed them and harassed them" (Judg 2:18).

Here we have the exact same word again. This does not mean that they went around, saying, "Ugh, how annoying! The enemy has entered the land!" No, just as in Exodus 2, it was a form of sighing, crying out and groaning which went up from their hearts to God and which produced deliverance. As a result of the people groaning and sighing, the land was delivered.

First Repentance

Travailing prayer will not come before you have prayed another type of prayer. First, you have to pray a prayer of repentance and devotion. The Bible says time and again, the children of Israel turned from God and sinned against Him. Then they regretted it and repented.

You cannot pray this type of prayer if you are not right with God. You must have committed yourself to Jesus and His will for your life. That is the requirement.

As soon as we start praying, we enter a battle in the spirit world. In every form of battle, the fact is that if you attack, the enemy counterattacks. The reason for this is that the enemy wants to keep you under his influence. All forms of war are really about two opponents who both want to dominate the other. We are in the kingdom of God, and the kingdom of God is not at peace with the kingdom of darkness. We are in a permanent state of war.

Speaking in geographical and political terms, war is really no less than a country wanting to exercise dominion over another country. The kingdom of God wants influence in this world. The kingdom of the enemy also wants influence. Satan exerts influence in this world and—as much as we allow him—also on the body of Christ. This means that when you and I start praying, God's kingdom starts wielding its influence.

You have to understand, that God hears your prayers. The Epistle of James says, *"The effective, fervent prayer of a righteous man avails much"* (Jam 5:16). When you, for instance, pray in tongues, your prayers whirl round in the spirit world and achieve far more than you perceive.

Exactly for this reason, the enemy is very frightened that you will start speaking in new tongues. He is afraid of you praying at all, but especially that you will pray in the spirit and speak in new tongues. He does everything to get you to stop doing it. He says, "What is this foolishness? To kick and wave your arms, hold your stomach and scream till your face turns red! It seems crazy!" And your mind thinks, "What *is* this? *I* have never prayed like this before."

At this point, it is necessary for you to understand that there are many different types of prayer. God wants to take you higher in the Spirit. This does not mean that you stop using your understanding, but it means that you learn to cooperate with the Spirit of God and with your inner being. If this is not clear to you, the enemy will pull you away from the supernatural. If you do that, you become a spectator, but God wants you to work together with Him, not only to watch.

The Spirit of God can be manifest in a number of different ways. First Corinthians 12 talks, among other things, about this. There is no limit to how many different ways the Spirit of God can reveal Himself. You cannot lock up the Spirit and say that He can only express Himself in a certain way. The Spirit of God does exactly as He pleases and He does it completely in accordance with the matter concerned and what has to be achieved. If the people of God are in captivity, the kind of prayer we call travailing prayer will deliver them and break down the opposition that is in the way.

Groans That Words Cannot Express

"In the same way, the Spirit helps us in our weakness. We do not know what we ought to pray for, but the Spirit himself intercedes for us with groans that words cannot express" (Rom 8:26 NIV).

Where we should pray, *what* we should pray, *how* we should pray and *when* we should pray—the Holy Spirit helps us with everything that has to do with prayer. He puts things on our hearts, which we then speak out in prayer to the Father in the name of Jesus. Prayer releases the power of God and God is given the liberty to work on this earth.

Many times you do not know what to pray. You do not really know what is happening in the spirit world and need to have it revealed to you. The Bible says that *"The Spirit himself intercedes for us with groans that words cannot express"*. So this is a type of prayer. We have read the words "sigh", "cry out" and "groan". The same word is used in Romans 8:26, *"groans that words cannot express"*. Your prayer surpasses what you know and reaches beyond, into that which only the Spirit of God knows.

When you pray in the Holy Spirit, your mind does not understand what you are doing, but often you know it in your spirit. Your spirit is like radar, and in your spirit you know what is going on. You have an approximate perception of what it is, but you may not be able to put your finger on it or with your understanding say exactly what it is. You learn to go beyond your limited understanding and work with the information that the Spirit of God has and which He deposits in your spirit. When this happens, groans that words cannot express will sometimes come forth—groans and wailings which are an expression of anguish, cries without words.

There is a fleshly, religious variation of this, which also needs to be mentioned. That is when it all becomes one great lamentation. You can hear if people are praying from their spirit or if it only is a religious disguise.

Some have difficulty speaking in tongues for a longer period of time because the enemy is constantly attacking their minds. The Holy Spirit wants to help each one to pray in this way. This type of prayer can change cities, families and even nations. It was a type of prayer Paul made use of all the time. On several occasions in the Epistle to the Galatians he expressed this. This entire epistle is really about prayer.

"Are you so foolish? Having begun in the Spirit, are you now being made perfect by the flesh? Have you suffered so many things in vain—if indeed it was in vain? Therefore He who supplies the Spirit to you and works miracles among you, does He do it by the works of the law, or by the hearing of faith?" (Gal 3:3-5)

After having begun in the Spirit, things started to go wrong for the Galatians. Then the Spirit of God came upon Paul and he started laboring for them.

"My little children, for whom I *labor* in birth again until Christ is formed in you" (Gal 4:19).

When Christ is formed in you, you start walking in liberty.

"It is for freedom that Christ has set us free. Stand firm, then, and do not let yourselves be burdened again by a yoke of slavery" (Gal 5:1 NIV).

Paul birthed the Galatians to liberty when he preached the Gospel to them and when he prayed for them. When they then took upon themselves new yokes of bondage, they went from being in the Spirit out into the flesh again. So Paul had to pray for them once again; he had to labor in birth for them, until Jesus Christ and his liberty once again was formed in them and the life of God flowed out of them.

Free to Follow the Holy Spirit

There is nothing that scares the enemy more than a believer who is free. It makes him nervous. If you are standing on the platform and the Holy Spirit says, "Lie down and pray to me!" you will do that immediately, if you are free. If you are not free you may say, "I can't do that. My trousers are newly freshly pressed and besides, we don't do that sort of thing around here. I have never done something like that before. And what will the preacher think?"

When such thoughts come to you and are allowed to freely exercise their influence, that is proof of you being in bondage. But if you pray, and Christ is allowed to be formed in you, you will be free in the Holy Spirit. This does not mean that you do a lot of crazy things all the time, but when the Holy Spirit wants to say or do something through you, you are free to be able to do it, your hands are not tied behind your back.

God wants you to come out into that freedom more and more. A type of prayer that produces this freedom in your life is groans that words cannot express. When the Holy Spirit intercedes for you, when He is allowed to take over and pray through you, groans without words will come from within you. It even exceeds what we normally would recognize as the gift of tongues. The prayer comes from deep within your spirit, from your inner being, and flows out of you. You pray, as some translations say, unarticulated tongues, with groans, with cries, with shouts.

It may bother your mind when you hear somebody praying in this way. The strangest noises come out and you think, "*what* is this? It cannot be prayer to sigh, cry and shout so violently. But it is prayer all the same.

Whenever the Spirit of God wants to show something or do something, odd things emerge at the same time. There will always be exaggerations. There will always be those who end up in a ditch. They find a nail and hammer it for the rest of their lives.

Prayer is so many different things and the Holy Spirit wants to help each one of us to enter a much deeper dimension of prayer. Travailing prayer is the Holy Spirit, giving birth to spiritual life in you.

Some have misunderstood this. Somebody wrote in an article, "They lie groaning on the platform, and then believe that people will be saved". Nobody has claimed that. What happens is that we plow up in the spirit world and pray forth things which later are manifested through the preaching of the Word.

Everything that Word of Life is and does today would not have existed, if we had not prayed in this manner. All work is birthed in this type of prayer. We have been criticized for praying like this, but we continue nevertheless, and we will continue doing it, because we have seen the results of it.

No Room For "Experts"

In 1981, God took my family and myself to Tulsa, USA. I ended up in a prayer group that prayed in the way I have been talking about. I did not understand a lot. They did not even take up prayer requests. I thought, "They probably do this for ten or fifteen minutes to loosen up the atmosphere. Then we will pray for other things." But one hour, two hours, three hours, four hours passed by and I thought, "Dear God, what is this?"

But I was hungry for God, and my attitude was that it does not matter if they stand on their hands and play the fiddle with their toes. If it works and if I just know it is of God, it can manifest itself in any way, I have no objections.

It felt very good on the inside, but my mind was like a beehive. I told God, "God, you have to tell me what this is." Then the Holy Spirit said, "Be quiet! When the time is right I will answer all your questions."

I was a part of that prayer group every week for half a year, before all my questions and objections were answered.

God showed me that I actually did not know a thing. We often appoint ourselves to be experts and believe that we know everything. In actual fact we know nothing. What do we know about angels? What do we know about the Holy Spirit? Sure, we have some knowledge of God, but there are tremendous dimensions and depths in the Holy Spirit which we have not even begun to discover. There is no room for "experts" who know everything in the kingdom of God.

The Spirit of God Comes as He Pleases

When the Holy Spirit comes upon us, the result is sometimes an unusual manifestation. Sometimes people start copying this. "Aha, that is what I am supposed to do!" It is not at all a sure thing that is what you are supposed to do. But if may well happen that the Spirit of God will come upon you in that way and *then* that is what you are to do.

Do not do a lot of odd things and think you are spiritual only because you shout loud enough or wave your arms about enough. But when the Spirit of God comes upon you, there are things you do in the Holy Spirit without really having a clue as to what it is. You only feel that you should do it and you know it is of God. The Holy Spirit does not come in the way we think He should come. He comes as He wishes.

As early as in the second verse of the Bible, we can read about the first revelation of the Holy Spirit. There it is said that the Spirit of God was hovering over the waters (Gen 1:2). That word means that the Spirit of God *broods*. It is the same word that has to do with sighing and groaning, and the same word Paul uses in his epistle to the Galatians.

The Importance of Obedience

Naaman, the leprous general from Syria, came to Elisha in order to be healed (2 King 5). But Elisha did not even come out to greet him, but sent a servant, somebody far below Naaman in dignity. This irritated Naaman exceedingly.

The servant said, "Wash yourself seven times in the Jordan, and you will be cleansed". This aggravated Naaman, "Would I wash myself seven times in a dirty river, when we have much better rivers at home!" Naaman became grumpy, angry and irritated. But he was still a leper.

Naaman's reasoning hindered him from being delivered. He had in advance decided *how* his healing would come about. This is the only time the Bible mentions somebody washing themselves in a river seven times. God never again healed in that way, but it was exactly what was needed to break Naaman's pride. When that obstacle was out of the way, he could cooperate with the Spirit of God in the supernatural.

Faith is obedience, and one does not argue with the Holy Spirit. You have to enter the life with God in which you do not constantly come with arguments of the soul. God is the one who has given you your understanding and He wants to use it, but there is a life in the Holy Spirit that has to take shape and be birthed in you. Then you can live in a liberty where the Spirit of God really can use you and you can hear from God—and not only from the enemy.

Travailing prayer produces that liberty. The enemy is scared stiff of you praying in this way, because he knows the liberty it achieves. This type of prayer—sighing, anguish, travailing prayer, groaning and crying out produced deliverance and freedom for the children of Israel. It also results in Christ being formed in you, even if there is anguish in the process itself.

There are unusual manifestations, which your understanding does not comprehend. You may be laying on the floor with somebody laying over you, crying, and you think it very embarrassing until it suddenly takes hold of your spirit and you start crying too. Carnal dams burst and the Spirit of God comes and washes you until you are clean and free.

The Initiative Comes From the Spirit of God

"When Jesus saw her (Mary) weeping, and the Jews who had come along with her also weeping, he was deeply moved in spirit and troubled" (John 11:33 NIV).

Notice where the initiative comes from. It comes from the Spirit of God in Jesus' spirit. Lazarus has died and Jesus is moved in His spirit and becomes troubled. He does not accept that Lazarus is dead. He wants life and deliverance.

We can pray in tongues and we can pray the prayer of travail on our own initiative, but there is a type of prayer we cannot enter into in just any way. The Spirit of God often comes with such prayer when people are ready and have a true longing. *"Deep calls to deep"* (Ps 42:7 NIV).

Jesus is moved in His spirit and troubled. In the New King James Version of the Bible, instead of the word "moved", the word "groaned" is used. In the original Greek, that is the same word that is repeatedly used on several occasions in Romans 8, where we read about "groans", "labor" and "groans that words cannot express". *That* is what Jesus is doing. He is not just irritated in general and upset because the circumstances are not as they should be,

116

but he groans from the depth of his spirit. He groans, labors and prays.

Jesus prays at least four different types of prayer before Lazarus is set free. He feels compassion in his spirit, he is moved in his spirit, he groans in the spirit and he commands and delivers. Here we also see how important it is that we are sensitive to what the Holy Spirit wants for the moment.

Perseverance is Required

"Then they brought to Him one who was deaf and had an impediment in his speech, and they begged Him to put His hand on him. And He took him aside from the multitude, and put His fingers in his ears, and He spat and touched his tongue. Then, looking up to heaven, He sighed, and said to him, 'Ephphatha,' that is, 'Be opened' (Mark 7:32-34).

Often we misunderstand what the Bible is saying because we have had our own human associations to the words. When you read that Jesus sighed, you may think that He was thinking, "Dear Father, what shall we do! God, do something, if You can!" It was not *that* type of sigh. It was prayer in the Holy Spirit—sighing, anguish and groaning in the Spirit—which came out of the spirit of Jesus and addressed the man, who was set free.

Much of what we want done—revival, healing and much more—will never be done unless we give ourselves to this type of prayer, and give ourselves to it for *more* than five minutes! You can pray for a short period of time or for longer. When Jesus prayed on this occasion, the prayer was probably quite short, but it came from the depth of his spirit and produced immediate results.

In Colossians we read that Epaphras, one of Paul's co-workers, goes through the same thing as Paul, when he prayed for the Galatians.

"Epaphras, who is one of you, a bondservant of Christ, greets you, always *laboring* fervently for you in prayers, that you may stand perfect and complete in all the will of God" (Col 4:12).

Epaphras wrestled, labored, suffered anguish and did battle for the Colossians. The word "labor" means to "work" or "toil". When a woman gives birth to a child, she is doing a work. It was the same type of work Paul, Epaphras and many of the others did in prayer. Paul says, *"My little children, for whom I labor in birth..."* (Gal 4:19). He means that he is in the same pain as a woman in labor. He has such a pain, he labors and *prays* as if he were in physical labor.

Pour Out Your Heart!

You will discover that the Old Testament—especially the Psalms—is full of verses about travailing prayer, verses you may not have noticed before now. We will look at some such Bible verses.

"Ask now, and see, whether a man is ever in labor with child? So why do I see every man with his hands on his loins like a woman in labor, and all faces turned pale?" (Jer 30:6).

This was a special type of prayer in an exceptional situation of distress. In this case they were just about losing hope, because Judah was so backslidden.

"Their heart cried out to the Lord, 'O wall of the daughter of Zion, let tears run down like a river day and night; give yourself no relief; give your eyes no rest. Arise, cry out in the night, at the beginning of the watches; pour out your heart like water before the face of the Lord. Lift your hands toward Him for the life of your young children, who faint from hunger at the head of every street'" (Lam 2:18-19).

The ones crying out are the ones who form the wall. The watchmen provide the protection. Prayer has a tremendous ability to protect and keep.

This is more than a quiet prayer with folded hands! Some say, "I pray loudly inside me." Yes, it is true that it says your *heart* cries out. That is inside you, but it also says for *you* to cry out: *"Arise, cry out!"* There is sighing, groaning, anguish, crying out and lamentation and there is crying. The Bible says you are to pour out your heart. It speaks of crying, *"let tears run down like a river..."* There are cries, loud cries before God. There is anguish, labor and wrestling.

"For we do not wrestle against flesh and blood, but against principalities, against powers, against the rulers of the darkness of this age, against spiritual hosts of wickedness in the heavenly places" (Eph 6:12).

The Greek word that is translated with "wrestle" really means "continuous wrestling". You are battling continuously, but not against flesh and blood—you are wrestling in the spirit world with your prayers. You are in anguish, you give birth to life, you shout and you cry before God. You pour out your heart, your spirit, your soul, your emotions. You let your tears run like a river. Your body is involved, you lift up your hands or you fall down on your face. Your entire being is involved, led by the Holy Spirit you do battle and wrestle in the spirit world and the result is deliverance for thousands of people.

This is prayer, that is not about you and "your little toe". It is about nations. It is about spiritual events. It is about stopping Satan's plans and opening up in the spirit for revival. It is about preparing the way for the return of the Lord, raising up the valleys and making low the mountains (Is 40:3-4). It is about praying for the daughter of Zion and her destruction (Lam 2:11). It is about changing the spiritual climate. This is what travailing prayer can achieve. It is the Holy Spirit doing battle through you.

What we call travailing prayer comprises groans, anguish, crying and battle. All prayer is a form of battle, but there is prayer which really is a battle of attack.

The Lord Roars From Zion

"The Lord also will roar from Zion, and utter His voice from Jerusalem; the heavens and earth will shake; but the Lord will be a shelter for His people, and the strength of the children of Israel" (Joel 3:16).

As believers, we can apply these promises to ourselves. If we are Zion, that means that we roar. We roar in two ways, because we have two means by which we can roar. One way is through proclamation. We roar when the Holy Spirit wants us to. We say when something is wrong and unrighteous. We proclaim the truth.

The second way in which we roar is through prayer. I have seen people be set completely free when I have prayed for them in the manner we have described here. It is nothing you can do in yourself. Then all it is, is a carnal yapping. But when Jesus, the Lion of Judah, emerges in us, there is no doubt or question.

There are many other types of prayer, but in this chapter I have wanted to create a greater understanding for the prayer we call travailing prayer. With groans, anguish, battle and wrestling in the Spirit we wage a form of war in which the Lord roars through us.

10

The Lord is a Warrior!

The Holy Spirit reveals Himself in various ways. He is wind, He is oil and He is fire. But He is also power. It is important to understand also that aspect. Some Christians do not, but take offense or become frightened when the power of the Holy Spirit comes up for discussion. But it is important not to exclude any of the manifestations of the Holy Spirit. It is better to flow with Him and receive Him in the way He comes for the moment.

There is something very offensive in God's nature, and you need to understand that aspect of God and learn how you can flow with it. If you do not do this, you will miss out on things God has planned for your life and the devil will be able to defeat you. There is no reason for you to let him win over you; you are to overcome him. Maybe you are thinking, "But the devil is already defeated." Sure, that is true, but in spite of this, he still makes trouble for you. For this reason you need to put him in his place, and you have to be very offensive when you come against him.

The Spirit of God can be very offensive, and as children of God we are expected to imitate our Father. The Bible says that God is a warrior: *"The Lord is a warrior; the Lord is his name"* (Ex 15:3 NIV). As God's children, we are like Him. This makes us warriors. Some are of the opinion that only a small number of Christians are warriors—prayer warriors—but that is incorrect. If you are born again, you are a soldier in the army of God.

"The Lord will march out like a mighty man, like a warrior he will stir up his zeal; with a shout he will raise the battle cry and will triumph over his enemies." (Is 42:13 NIV),

I know that many become nervous when we shout, jump and cry out. But if my God in heaven roars, I will roar. In Joel 3:16 we read that the Lord roars from Zion. If He roars and I am His child, I have nothing against giving a little roar myself.

"But it could be of the flesh," some object. Sure, everything can be done in the flesh, but it can also be done in the spirit. Which spirit do you have on the inside? You have the Spirit of God—if you are born again. God's Spirit is God. If God is a warrior, then also that aspect of God is on the inside of you, through His Spirit. God's Spirit in you wants to wage war against the devil, our enemy. The state is not our enemy, the press is not our enemy. No, the devil is our enemy, and we need to learn how to wage war and do battle against him. If all you do is holler and scream, you have gotten stuck in yet another pattern. That is not what we are talking about. We are talking about freedom to let the Spirit of the Lord have free reign for what He wants to do, without us limiting Him with our intellect or our traditions.

Parade or Real War?

We have some "war songs" we like to sing. But sometimes it becomes more like a parade than a real war. Parades are delightful and impressive. Of course it makes an impression to see lots of uniformed, medal-adorned soldiers marching along with weapons in their hands—but that is not war, but a parade. You are not called to march in a parade. Sometimes it is almost as if we are doing just that in our services. We have brought our weapons, and we swing them in the air. Everybody thinks it is wonderful: "Here comes the army, give them a hand!" That can be quite all right now and then, for there is a time for such things also. But do you know where the army really belongs? Out in the mud and down in the trenches. If you cannot handle being be there, something is wrong somewhere. God wants to put in you an ability to endure sufferings as a good soldier in Jesus Christ.

You cannot allow yourself only to be feeble. You cannot wish to constantly be patted on the back. Yes, there is a place in God, where you can enjoy his compassion and love, but God's love is always joined with truth. There is no love without truth, just as there is no faith without obedience.

This means that if you flee truth and at the same time ask for love, it is not agape love—the type of love which sets people free—that you want. It is a carnal, sentimental and fleshly kind of love, which actually only wants to hinder you from moving on in the spirit. Whether you are an average believer or a minister, you have to be able to see the difference and use the sword of the Spirit against every type of falsification.

We are creatures created by love and we walk in the love of God, but when that love flows out of us and meets evil, it will be revealed as pure hate against the enemy.

In the Right Element

Before Man fell into sin, God said something wonderful to us. He said that we were to go out and fill the earth, dominate it and subdue it (Gen 1:28). Just as the birds are created to fly and the fish to swim, we are created in the image of God to rule and conquer. I am not referring to the Great Commission in which Jesus gave us authority in His name to go out into all the world and win it. No, here I am referring to the act of creation.

God created the fish for swimming. Water is its right element. If you take a fish out of the water it will be in the wrong element. God created the birds to fly. If you lower a bird into the water and try to get it to swim there, it will not come off very well. It is in the wrong element. Similarly, God created each one of us. He created us to walk in rule and authority and for this reason He imparted this to our spirits and our entire beings.

God called the human race to go out and possess, conquer, dominate and subdue the earth. This is the initial calling of the human race and it has been laid down on the inside of us. It is also in people who have not been born again—it is in all of us. But the devil is out to oppress this God-given instinct, in people in general, and particularly in believers.

Your enemy, the devil, will always fight your authority. He hates authority. He cannot stand it, because he is full of rebellion and does all he can to take your authority away from you. If he can get you to sin or rebel or if he can get you to compromise, he can steal this rule and authority from you. But if you do not listen to him, if you do not give in to the devil, if you do not worship him through compromise or sin, you can walk in that authority all your life. But one thing is certain—you will not be popular with the devil.

We believe in favor with God, for it is biblical, and we also believe in favor with people. But we do not believe in favor with the devil nor with his followers.

"But I have great favor with non-Christians," somebody might say.

That is not the question. God's grace and the Holy Spirit on the inside of us attracts non-believers. We are in this world in order to evangelize. What I am saying is that there always will be a measure of persecution against you, if you follow God.

We are definitely not supposed to have some kind of persecution-mania, but we are expected to be have joy in the battle. When the devil attacks you from the left and the right because you are a child of the living God, the Lord, our Warrior, it is time for you to shout hallelujah and start fighting back.

I have never understood pastors who are afraid of persecution. I cannot understand that anybody, who is called to be on the front line in the army of God can be scared of battle. I am not talking about creating persecution or believing God for it, but God has promised that if you obey Him there will come a certain measure of persecution against you.

Joy in the Battle

When we founded Word of Life Church many people said, "If you only would not shout so loudly in tongues, you would attract more people. If you would not jump around and dance and run around like you do, more people would come to your meetings."

Sure, there are excesses everywhere, but because of fear of excess, many servants of the Lord have lost the strength and anointing in their ministries. Do not be afraid of excesses. Allow the Holy Spirit to come as powerfully as He wishes and bless people, when you hold meetings.

I am so happy we did not yield to these suggestions and compromise. Instead we have seen abundant fruit. In ten years' time, more than 7200 students have attended one or two years at our Bible School. Now they are spread out all over Scandinavia and many other parts of the world. Many are full of the fire of God and do battle with joy in the

Holy Spirit, for no one has taught them that could be wrong.

If you are a pastor, you have to realize that God has not called you to hide behind the troops. You are to run first. As a pastor and leader, you are to be the wildest and most fanatic of all. You are an example to your church. They look to you and follow you.

There is a joy in the battle. There is joy and satisfaction in casting demons out of people. We have had visits from people who have come to us from other Christian denominations, just to be set free from evil spirits. Nobody in their church thought it could be demons or knew how to take care of the problem. It is a shame that people should have to live with such problems without getting any help.

Love Righteousness—Hate Wickedness

"And I will put enmity between you and the woman, and between your offspring and hers; he will crush your head, and you will strike his heel." (Gen 3:15 NIV)

When humanity fell into sin, God proclaimed war on Satan. This war has been going on since then. We know that Jesus won the victory in this battle on Calvary. But the war is in one sense still not finished, because we are still proclaiming this victory and we are still winning territory.

From this first episode, when God proclaimed war, there has been a constant war. Virtually from the first to last page in the Bible we see a war in progress. It is no small side issue; it is something that concerns us all. For this reason, we all need to know how we are to conduct ourselves as soldiers in the army of God.

In Judges, we read of a man called Samson. When we hear his name mentioned we often think of failure. We think of how he fell and lost the anointing which was upon his life. But Samson also did a lot of good and performed mighty deeds. He was anointed by God. Judges 13:25 says, *"And the Spirit of the Lord began to move upon him at Mahaneh Dan between Zorah and Eshtaol"*. Then, in chapter 14:4 we read something very interesting, *"But his father and mother did not know that it was of the Lord – that he was seeking an occasion to move against the Philistines. For at that time the Philistines had dominion over Israel"*.

God hates it when the devil has the advantage over the people of God. Hebrews 1:9 says that Jesus Christ loves righteousness and hates wickedness. The Spirit of God loves the truth. He loves people, but He hates the devil and He hates wickedness. God hates His enemies. That is a fact we can never disregard.

Some people preach that we all can have a second chance, a third chance and a fourth chance. But we can never forget that sin always has consequences, even if they do not thwart the grace of God. God restored David after he had committed adultery with Bathsheba, but there were things David had to fight throughout his life because of that sin. There is no cheap grace, where you can do what you want, with the idea that you can come back to God as if nothing has happened and that God would turn a blind eye to everything you have done.

Naturally, God will restore you if you have genuine repentance in your heart. If you repent, if you cry out for the grace of God as David did, God will restore you and establish you in your position once again. He will no longer remember the sin you committed. But the consequences remain. A process has been started. There is a law of sowing and reaping, and it applies to all areas of life. But thank God, God is greater than the circumstances and can perform miracles.

Something which needs to be emphasized much more in the body of Christ today is the fear of the Lord. The believers need to have such a fear of the Lord that they do not even dare think about anything unclean because they know that a judgement will come. "Will God condemn me?" you might ask. No, but he will judge you. If you are a child of God you will get to heaven, but as for me it is not the only thing I want. I want to run my course. I want to finish my race. I want to do everything God expects of me, while I am on this earth. Therefore I had better not compromise, try to please people or speak that which tickles their ears. I had better do that which Jesus has commanded me to do.

When you do what God has called you to do, and when anointing for the ministry comes upon your life, the devil will come against you. Then you need to see that God has put you where you are because he is "seeking an occasion to move against the Philistines".

God Wants the Church to Have an Influence

When we started our work in Uppsala and started to go out into Scandinavia and Europe, we were met with very strong reactions through newspapers and television. A lot of trash was thrown at us and some preachers came to us and said, "Take it a bit easy. You do not need to preach so sharply." I asked the Lord about this and He said, "You are not preaching sharply enough!"

Now we are not talking about being harsh. We are talking about doing what God wants, without compromising. The ways of the Lord are not always the same as the ways of people, and His thoughts are not the thoughts of men. It is better that we move up to God's level than try to pull Him down to our level.

If our country's government tells us that we cannot do what the Word of God tells us to do, we say, "Sorry! We obey you, but not when what you say contradicts the Word of God."

When attacks from the mass media were at their worst, the Spirit of the Lord said, "The trash they are throwing at you, will become a great heap, and from that platform you will be able to speak to the nation."

The Lord said this some years ago. Since then we have seen it happen. Today we are speaking to the nation. On May 20 1990, the first live TV-service was broadcast from Word of Life, on the state-owned television station, which still have monopoly on television in Sweden. We know that several people were saved, healed and encouraged in their faith through this service. Many people all over the country, who knew of our church through the mass media, started seeing us in a new light.

The devil tried to stop us from being devoted and committed. He tried to get us to become insignificant, backslidden Christians. When we did not want to give in to this, he said, "Okay, then you will be a small crazy sect. Nobody will listen to you. Fewer and fewer will come to your meetings and you will be crazy in the eyes of the world." But this is not what happened. The fact, you see, is that there is no limit to what God can do for you, if you simply do not compromise.

When the Spirit of God is seeking an occasion to move against somebody, as he did against the Philistines, God is seeking an opportunity for revenge. Then you had better be in the center of His will. The Spirit of God today, is seeking an opportunity to knock out the devil and raise up His Church again, so that it becomes what it is destined to be. The Church is called to win the lost, to build up the believers, to rule over the spiritual atmosphere and to prophesy to governments and nations.

The devil does not like the fact that the Church has influence in the spiritual atmosphere. The Lord told us, that if we only would continue moving forwards with boldness, we would see the spiritual atmosphere in our nation change. This is exactly what has happened. Today everybody is talking about religion. One reason is that God has used us to draw attention to it. Today we have the attention of the people. Now that we have their attention we need to reach them with salvation also. We have not reached that point yet, but we are getting there. Everybody will hear the Gospel.

The devil would prefer to see us Christians sitting frightened in a corner. But remember what Jesus did. He left the insignificant Nazareth and settled in Capernaum. Capernaum was located by the Sea of Galilee and was a central town in Galilee—a commercial town, a chief town for many different enterprises. The first thing that happened was that an evil spirit manifested itself—in the synagogue! The spirit cried out saying, *"Let us alone! What have we to do with You, Jesus of Nazareth? Did You come to destroy us? I know who You are—the Holy One of God!' But Jesus rebuked him, saying, 'Be quiet, and come out of him!'"* (Mark 1:24-25).

Jesus took command. He took charge of the territory and that is what God wants us to do too. In order to do this, we need the Holy Spirit. We need the spirit of ruling, of power and warfare, which was upon Samson and upon Jesus. When that spirit came over Samson he tore the lion to pieces. Similarly, you can tear "lions"—attacks—to pieces, when the Holy Spirit comes upon you. It is this Spirit and this power which makes the devil flee. The Holy Spirit drives him out of areas and territories which he has controlled for a long time or from people he has held captive.

Hold on to Your Weapons!

We have been equipped with weapons. In 2 Corinthians 10:3-4 we read, *"For though we walk in the flesh, we do not war according to the flesh. For the weapons of our warfare are not carnal but mighty in God for pulling down strongholds..."*

If you do not have any weapons, you cannot fight. For this reason, the devil's number one goal is to keep you in ignorance of which weapons you have and to scare you from using them. This is why one often gets to hear, when somebody starts praying strongly and loudly in the spirit, "Shush, not so loud!" This is inspired by evil spirits who seek to control.

We know that oddities can occur where speaking in tongues is concerned, just as where prophecies are concerned, but that is nothing to be afraid of. If people become muddled and start doing bizarre things, you can correct them, so that they come up out of the ditch again. We can never let fear of the supernatural seize us. God has given us a tremendous weapon though the gift of speaking in other tongues.

You speak in tongues in order to edify yourself, worship God, protect yourself and attack the enemy. Speaking in tongues is a spiritual weapon, a spiritual weapon you do battle with. The devil would like you never to use this weapon. Instead, he would like to take it from you. But God wants you to have the gift of tongues, use it, increase in knowledge about it and become more and more proficient in using it.

Liberty is the best advantage you can have over your enemy. If you cannot move freely in an army, if you are not flexible, so that you can act quickly and surprise the enemy, you are lost. You will not win any battles. Therefore, you must make sure you guard your freedom.

Ways of guarding one's freedom is to pray in the spirit, dance before the face of God in praise and worship, lie on one's face, shouting and crying out in travailing prayer and pouring out one's heart before God. If you do that without being ashamed, you will enter into a greater freedom. You will fight more battles for the Lord and win far more victories.

Time For Battle

The Bible says that there is *"a time for war and a time for peace"* (Eccl 3:8 NIV). The time of war will come before the time of peace. The time of peace is the Millennium. Now we are at war. God will revive you so that you become aware of this, become activated in your inner being and in that way become a mighty warrior.

Do you know who is on the inside of you, if you are born again? The Lion of Judah. The lion is a unique animal. Twenty-two hours of the day it lies sleeping. It does nothing, just *is* a lion. It does not run around, roaring at everything that moves—as some Christians do. But when the Holy Spirit comes upon us and urges us to battle, we are prepared to fight anything. You are as a lion; you have the same spirit. It is on the inside of you and you do not need get into the right mood to be able to fight.

"As a lion roars, and a young lion over his prey (When a multitude of shepherds is summoned against him, he will not be afraid of their voice nor be disturbed by their noise)..." (Is 31:4).

Do not be frightened by the voices that are raised against the Lord. You do not need to be afraid of anything. You can walk through this life without being restrained by fear.

Be bold! Live as a lion, roar and keep going. Do not suppress it, but let God refine it so that the devil does not take the weapons out of your hand. We need God's power, might and glory, in order to chase away the devil and see the kingdom of God be spread.

Actively seek God, and a spirit of faith, a spirit of victory, a spirit of warfare and a spirit of breakthrough will come upon your life. The spirit of boldness, the spirit of intercession and the spirit of perseverance will make you a strong warrior who, in the strength of the Lord, will have many victories, much joy—and who will see many people be set free and changed. *"The Lord is with you, mighty warrior"* (Judg 6:12 NIV).

Books by Ulf Ekman

A Life of Victory
The guidance, help and inspiration you need to put God's Word first. Fifty-four chapters, each dealing with a particular area of the believer's life. *288 pages.*

The Apostolic Ministry
How do we recognise an Apostle? What role does the Apostle have? What can we learn from the life of Paul, the greatest Apostle? Ulf Ekman gives Biblical guidance in this book. *128 pages.*

The Authority in the Name of Jesus
When you receive a revelation of what the name of Jesus really means, you will have boldness like never before. *Booklet, 32 pages.*

The Church of the Living God
The Church of the Living God is something far beyond what we think or experience. It is the place where the End-time Revival will have its source and climax—and you have a place in that Church. *158 pages.*

Destined for Victory
God has victorious plans for you. His plans never fail! In this book you will discover: • How to aviod fear of failure • How to withstand the attacks of Satan • How spiritual laws operate and • How Gods Word always brings results. *Booklet, 32 pages.*

Destroy the Works of the Devil
Jesus came to earth to destroy the works of the devil. His death on the cross struck Satan a death blow. Jesus triumphed over him and won the victory for YOU! *Booklet, 32 pages.*

Doctrine—The Foundations of the Christian Faith
Ulf Ekman gives an objective and biblical account of each fundamental doctrine of the Christian faith. In days when the Christian message is increasingly diluted and twisted *Doctrine* will be an asset for every pastor, leader and believer. *256 pages.*

Faith that Overcomes the World
Explains how faith arises, how it becomes operational, and what makes it grow. *144 pages.*

Financial Freedom
A thorough, biblical study on money, riches and material possessions. *128 pages.*

God is a Good God
God has given you abundantly more than you can ever grasp for your entire lifetime. This book examines God's character and nature, and reveals His overflowing love for you. *Booklet, 32 pages.*

God, the State and the Individual
God not only deals with individuals, but with nations and governments. You can change the destiny of your nation! *112 pages.*

God Wants to Heal Everyone
Discover the wonderful fact that God's will is to heal everyone—including you. *Booklet, 32 pages.*

The Holy Spirit
The Holy Spirit is your guide, your teacher, your counselor and your helper.
Discover how you can live each day in the power of the Holy Spirit.
Booklet, 32 pages.

I Found my Destiny
Follow Ulf Ekman from his boyhood home in Gothenburg to "Livets Ord" –
Word of Life Church in Uppsala, Sweden. From 1983 until today Word of Life
has become a center for education, evangelism, mission and reformation in
Sweden and throughout the world. *150 pages.*

Jesus Died for You
Blessing is a daily reality when you understand the power of the cross:
• Satan's plans were crushed • Sickness was defeated • Poverty was broken
• Depression turned to joy. *Booklet, 32 pages.*

The Jews—People of the Future
Clarifies basic truths about the people and the land. Historical facts and biblical
prophecies combine to reveal the fulfillment of God's End-time Plan. *160 pages.*

The Power in the New Creation
A new dimension of victorious living awaits you. The Lord is with you, Mighty
Warrior! *Booklet, 32 pages.*

Prayer Changes Nations
Ulf Ekman teaches here on what characterizes the time before revival, the
work that needs to be done and how the Holy Spirit can change every believer
into a bold prayer-warrior. *156 pages.*

The Prophetic Ministry
"Provides essential guideposts for the operation of the prophetic ministry
today." From the Foreword by Demos Shakarian. *224 pages.*

Available from your local Christian bookstore, or order direct from the publisher:

Sweden: Word of Life Publications
P.O. Box 17, S-751 03, Uppsala, Sweden. Telephone +46 18 16 14 00
Fax +46 18 69 31 90. E-mail order@livetsord.se

Australia: Ulf Ekman Ministries
P.O. Box 2324 Mansfield Qld. 4122. Telephone/fax +61 73 849 53 25.
E-mail australia@ulfekman.org

UK: Word of Life Sweden
P.O. Box 70, Edenbridge, Kent TN8 5ZG UK. Telephone +44 1732 86 71 71
Fax +44 1732 86 71 11. E-mail uk@ulfekman.org

USA: Ulf Ekman Ministries
P.O. Box 700717, Tulsa, OK 74170, USA. Telephone +1 918 488 0881
Fax +1 918 488 0906 Toll free # 1 800 428 1760.
E-mail usa@ulfekman.org

Canada: Ulf Ekman Ministries
P.O. Box 66058 Heritage Postal Outlet, Edmonton, Alberta, T6J 6T4 Canada.
Telephone +1 403 887 3313 Fax +1 403 887 3355.
E-mail canada@ulfekman.org

Word of Life
P.O. Box 17
S-751 03
Uppsala
Sweden

Word of Life

The Vision that God gave for the work at Word of Life, Uppsala, Sweden is:

Equip my people with My word of faith.
Show them their spiritual weapons.
Teach them how to use them, and
Send them out into victorious battle for the Lord!

If you want to know more about Word of Life, fill in this form, send it to us, and we will supply you with further information free of charge.

☐ Yes, I would like to receive Word of Life Newsletter free of charge.

☐ Yes, I would like to receive information about Word of Life Bibleschool.

☐ Yes, I would like to receive Word of Life Product Catalogue.

Name: ....

Address: ....

State: .... Country: ....

Zip Code: .... Telephone: ....

Word of Life, P.O. Box 17, S-751 03 Uppsala, Sweden. Telephone +46 18 16 14 00,
Telefax +46 18 69 31 90. E-mail info@livetsord.se, Homepage: www.livetsord.se